M000238444

SMART TECHNOLOGY OPTIMIZES YOUR PERFORMANCE
THE POWER TO RUN

Authors: Hans van Dijk, Ron van Megen,
Koen de Jong
The Power to Run
smart technology optimizes your performance
The Choir Press, first edition April 2022.
Keywords: running, jogging, sports, physiology,
power, running power meters, wattage.

ISBN print: 978-1-78963-280-4
ISBN eBook: 978-1-78963-285-9

Parts of this book have been published earlier
in the books The fastest way to your next Personal Best: Running Power and The Secret of
Running; or in one of the many articles by the
authors published in running magazines and on
websites.

Cover design: Femke Hoogland
Cover image: Andrew T. Foster
Inside cover: Femke Hoogland
Photos: Janneke Poort, Pixabay.com,
istockphoto.com, Ron van Megen, TUI Sports,
Guido Vroemen, Giancarlo Colombo, Harry van
't Veld, Kistler
Publisher: The Choir Press

© MMXXII Hans van Dijk, Ron van Megen, Koen
de Jong, NedRUN

No part of this publication may be reproduced and / or
made public in any way or in any medium whatsoever
without the prior written consent of the authors. Written
permission is not required if it can be demonstrated that
the book contributed to a PB in the 5K, 10K, half or full
marathon, in which case sharing is welcome.

Disclaimer: We've compiled the book with great care
and have written it with great pleasure and dedication.
We don't believe there is anything in the book that
could harm our readers, but still should note that we as
authors are not responsible for any risk or loss that may
be incurred by the contents of this book.

SMART TECHNOLOGY OPTIMIZES YOUR PERFORMANCE
THE POWER TO RUN

PRACTICAL TIPS AND CASES

Part V: Applications in practice

Afterword

Foreword

by Koen de Jong

Years ago, coach and sports physician Guido Vroemen spoke enthusiastically about power measurement for runners. I wasn't very interested. I preferred to train mostly without equipment and, whenever I did want to use some sort of measuring device, I just used a basic heart rate monitor.

With a heart rate monitor, I gained insight about my body (heart rate) instead of my output (power). For that matter, I didn't believe that you could accurately measure power in running. As a cyclist, I could somewhat imagine measuring power output, but as a runner, it seemed unreliable and pointless.

Until, that is, I bumped into data geeks Hans van Dijk and Ron van Megen -- engineers who love running and measuring running. The duo were very enthusiastic about Stryd's running power meter and it caught my attention. I tried to read their book The Secret of Running, but it proved to be a challenge. As it turned out, the book is full of formulas like

$$t = E/P = mgh/P = m*9.81*100/P = 981/(P/m).$$

Halfway through the first chapter, I set the book aside. Too complicated. I just wanted to run and to find out how to improve my 10K PB. Or, how to run a full marathon and set a realistic time goal.

I emailed Hans and Ron asking if they would like to get a cup of coffee. Partially because their contagious enthusiasm for running by power made me curious about this new phenomenon, but I also wondered whether it was a good idea for me, historically a "run-by-feel" athlete, to run by power.

Hans and Ron laughed when I "complained" about their book. "Yes, we love formulas and calculations," admitted Hans.

"But you don't have to make it that complicated," Ron added. "Running power is very simple. Easier than running with a heart rate monitor."

At first I didn't believe them. But after two coffees, an orange juice, and a lengthy discussion on power, I wanted to try it. I followed the instructions Ron and Hans gave me and started training by power. And to my surprise, it brought a lot of peace to my training. Running by power does indeed appear to give more peace than running on heart rate.

Peace?

I didn't expect that. I thought that adding something else on top of heart rate, Strava, and GPS, would be overwhelming. But it turns out that I now only have to pay attention to one thing: my power. My power fluctuates much less than my heart rate, it is very reproducible, and, to my surprise, it turns out to work really well: I've been consistently getting faster ever since I started to run with a power meter.

In this book Hans van Dijk, Ron van Megen, and I write about the pros and cons of running by power. Runners who've been training by power for some time share their experiences. And we'll discuss in detail the differences between training by heart rate, pace, or power.

Initially, our goal was to write a book about running power in the general sense. We didn't want to write a refined brochure about Stryd, the best-known power meter on the market. This edition contains experiences with Stryd because they are the current market leader, and by a significant margin.

With this book and any power meter, training will be easier than ever. You don't need an expensive personal trainer and you don't have to do an exercise test every few months. With your running power meter, you can easily go full throttle once a month on your favorite (short) distance and your data will automatically remain up-to-date and reliable.

If you're running with a power meter, you have your coach on your shoe, and every session is automatically included in your training analysis.

All you have to do: train with variety, and enjoy your new PBs.

In this book I regularly draw on my own experiences for the question "What's In It For You". The knowledge and "Backgrounds" about running by power as well "Practical Tips and Cases" come mainly from Hans van Dijk and Ron van Megen. We tried to write a book for runners who want to improve themselves. Regardless of whether you want to run a 20 or 30 minute 5K, whether you train to race 10K, or you run for general health.

Running power is a valuable tool from the moment you decide to pursue greater fitness. I even suspect that within five years, running power will be more common than heart rate training is today.

Not sure if running power is right for you? This book will help you find the answer to that. Have fun reading and running.

Hans van Dijk en Ron van Megen

Preface

Running by power is not yet commonplace among runners. In October 2019, I ran the Amsterdam marathon with a Stryd power meter, and it was the first time that I ever measured my power while running. I had no idea what to do with it! I had done my training with a heart rate monitor, so I had reliable heart rate targets that I knew could lead me to a PB. Still, I clicked a power meter on my shoe to measure my power.

During the marathon I did nothing with the values, but after my conversations with Ron van Megen and Hans van Dijk I became curious, and the measurements of an entire marathon seemed like a valuable starting point. After the race, I checked the Stryd app and learned that I had averaged 229 Watts.

Neat.

But I still didn't do anything with it yet. I enjoyed my shiny new PB (2:59:02) and took a month of rest.

At the end of my month off I started to experiment with training by power. I learned what my power values were for a 5K, a 10K, a half marathon, and a full marathon. I learned which Power Zone I should target for my interval training and what power target I could maintain for my endurance runs. It turns out to be amazingly simple. I didn't need the formulas used by Ron van Megen and Hans van Dijk in The Secret of Running unless I wanted more background information. All I really need to know is: what is my power target for today? And my power meter gives me a simple answer to that.

I regularly speak to other runners who also train by power. Two comments keep coming back for all runners: "It gives me peace of mind" and "I've made enormous progress."

Everyone I speak to who has trained with power for a few months is enthusiastic. But the runners who don't train with power have many questions. And doubts. These are all questions and doubts that I have had myself. Some I've heard include "Isn't training by heart rate more reliable?", "How do you measure progress and recovery?", "Isn't it complicated?", and "How do you determine the right power target to train with?"

With this book, we want to explain the pros and cons of running with power. Armed with this knowledge, you can decide for yourself whether running with power is right for you.

Note. We write in this book about power and how you can train smarter by running with power. If you want to train with power after reading this book, you'll need a power meter. At the moment, only Stryd's power meter is reliable. Nowadays, well-known brands such as Polar, Garmin and Coros, and apps for Apple Watch and iPhone, all do something with power. But as mentioned, the capabilities from these alternatives are not yet accurate enough, and they are less suitable for real training.

Ron, Hans, and I, therefore, are in close contact with Stryd. The openness with which they provide answers to our questions is always stimulating. We're very enthusiastic about their meter and the possibilities. We also expect more good power meters to appear on the market in the coming years. Ron and Hans test all new meters and write about their findings on their website https://theSecretofRunning.com. So, should a power meter come onto the market that is just as reliable as Stryd, you'll read it there first.

WHAT'S
IN IT
FOR YOU

What is power exactly, and why should you measure it?

1.1 What are Watts?

After many poor grades and frustrating struggles, I was happy to be able to drop physics in the ninth grade of high school. I'll take languages over the hard sciences any day!

What I am interested in (in addition to languages) is running, making how to progress transparent, and finding ways to improve my sports performance.

To train with power, you don't even need to know what Watts are. Even without knowing, you can improve personal records and make progress. For example, you don't need to know how the Internet works to use it. If you know to enter the URL for your favorite news website, you'll automatically see the news of the day, even without knowing how it's possible that you can access the Internet from nearly any place in the world. It's exactly the same with wattage from your running power. You can work with it, without knowledge of power itself and without knowledge of how power is measured. As long as you know at what level of power you have to run in a workout, or at what level of power you can run during a 5K, 10K, or half or full marathon, you will make progress.

If you're not interested in the basic information of Watts and power, but just want to do targeted training for your PB, you can skip Part I of this book and scroll straight to Part II. There, we explain how you can use your power to improve your running performance.

If you're not yet convinced of the usefulness of power training, it's instructive to know what power meters actually measure, how they do it, and what the differences are with heart rate measurement.

A Watt is a physical unit of measurement used to indicate power, which is the amount of energy consumed per second. Energy is represented by the unit Joule. Calories may be something you are familiar with from food. Joules are simply an alternative way to represent energy. Let's take a look at some energy and power values that we may be familiar with. A kcal is equal to 4.184 kilojoules. Nutritionists tell us that we consume (roughly) 2500 kcal per day, which corresponds to 10,460 kJ. In addition to kcal and kJ, we also recall energy consumption as kilowatt hours (kWh) when tracking use of electricity. 1 kWh equals 3600 kJ. So, we can say that the energy value of our daily food corresponds to 10,460 / 3,600 = 2.9 kWh. That's not much. Especially when we consider that 1 kWh costs approximately $0.135. If we were to eat electricity, we would only need to pay 2.9 * 0.135 = $0.39 to cover our needs each day.

How do we make use of this knowledge?

In his article appearing in Outside, author Alex Hutchinson nicely describes why we're all interested in calories, even if we just don't know it yet. Why should you care? It's a matter of terminology, says Hutchinson. If you do a sports performance test having your VO_2 max determined with advanced equipment, you're actually also measuring calories. Oxygen uptake is measured, as it's a good measure of energy consumption. And if you use this data to determine your heart rate zones and where your anaerobic threshold is, then you use your heart rate as a proxy for energy use; in other words, calories. And even for runners who run by feel (without a heart rate monitor), you could argue that they rely on their perception of how quickly they burn calories and how long they last. In short: knowing your use of calories plays a big role in your preparation for a new PB.

When we run, a chain reaction of physical activities takes place. Our heart rate increases, our lung capacity is used to a greater extent, our muscles are switched on, and blood flow accelerates. You can think of the human body as a complex miracle where 100,000 billion cells intelligently work together. But you can also represent the function of the human motor, the muscles and the heart-lung function, which can deliver a certain power, in a number expressed in Watts.

We all know that running takes energy. And it makes sense that it takes more energy to run a marathon as fast as possible, than it does to run 5 kilometers at ease. You can express the energy you use in kilojoules, or kJ.

Watts are the number in which your energy consumption per second is expressed. You can imagine a runner as a machine that extracts energy from food and converts it into valuable fuels for running. There is one problem: no machine is perfectly efficient, and neither is your body. You never get as much energy from your body as you put into it. For example, a car is only 25% efficient. If your car has used 100 joules of gasoline energy, only 25 of these joules have been used to propel the car forward, while the remaining 75 joules have been converted to useless heat.

Your muscles are also around 25% efficient, under normal circumstances. But that depends, among other things, on training, stride length, ground contact time, temperature, and more.

Together with your weight, your energy consumption and your power are therefore a golden combination to predict how fast you can run at certain distances. Because, if you know how much power your body can deliver, you also know what your body can do to push your weight in a given direction at a certain speed.

> ### *"Power is the amount of energy per second it takes to propel your body in a particular direction"*

Ron and Hans have created a clear model to describe running power:

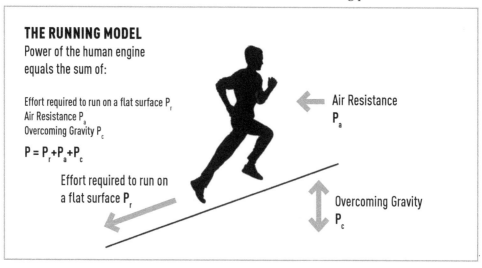

THE RUNNING MODEL
Power of the human engine
equals the sum of:

Effort required to run on a flat surface P_r
Air Resistance P_a
Overcoming Gravity P_c

$$P = P_r + P_a + P_c$$

Effort required to run on
a flat surface P_r

Air Resistance P_a

Overcoming Gravity P_c

Figure 1: The Running Model

This model looks simple, but is based on complicated formulas. For example, the air resistance depends on, among other things, wind speed, temperature, air pressure, height above sea level, and your body size. You'll also notice that the air resistance is different when you run alone or in a group, where you're (partially) sheltered from air flows.

The North Sea Half Marathon is the most famous half marathon in the Netherlands. You start on the beach near Amsterdam, and halfway, you turn off the beach, back through the dunes. A very tough section, where the runners on the beach were facing strong winds, however was an excellent opportunity for Hans and Ron to test the Stryd power meter in strong winds. A running friend of theirs - Niels - ran this section of North Sea Half Marathon with Stryd, and the results were interesting.

What happened?

On the beach and running against strong wind, it turned out that Niels had to deliver an average of 40 Watts to overcome the wind while running, Defying power peaks of more than 70 Watts. Running with a constant power, you can imagine that your speed will be quite a lot slower if the wind alone requires an extra 40 Watts to overcome. Niels ran consistently at 270 Watts, a wattage that he knew he could sustain for a half marathon. His pace was 8:05 min/mile in the strong headwind and (with the same power!) as compared to the pace he ran with a tailwind, that being 7:00 min/mile. His run time: 1:36:28. By running with constant power, he knew exactly what to do in the strong wind. If he was measuring heart rate, this wouldn't have worked in the changing wind gusts, because heart rate always needs a little time to climb to a steady and reliable number. Running with pace would not have been possible at all, because he could never have known how much slower he'd have to run against the headwind. This example clearly shows how running with power works well in strong winds (and also on hilly terrain).

This model looks simple, but is based on complicated formulas. For example, the air resistance depends on, among other things, wind speed, temperature, air pressure, height above sea level, and your body size. You'll also notice that the air resistance is different when you run alone or in a group, where you're (partially) sheltered from air flows.

The great thing about power is this: all these conditions can be captured in only one single number: your power. And if you know at what level of power you need to run to get better, you will improve quickly.

RUNNING WITH POWER

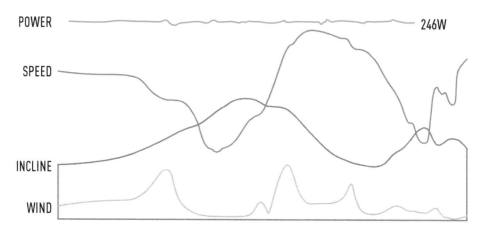

Figure 2: Running with Power: one number

Altitude, wind, temperature, speed, heart rate, and air pressure: all of these variables affect the total time of a race. Of course, you can't constantly keep an eye on all of these variables. When the weather gets warmer or when you run up a hill or a bridge, it affects your heart rate and your pace. Should you mainly pay attention to your heart rate or your pace? And in warmer weather, is it better to run with a higher heart rate, a lower heart rate, or the same heart rate you run with in cold weather? These questions are difficult to answer. And, during a race, it's too complicated to take all of these variables into account. The big advantage of running with power is that you only have to keep an eye on this one simple to understand number that takes everything into account: altitude, temperature, speed, wind, humidity, and air pressure. The graph above clearly shows the benefits of running with power. While all variables can freely change, you can simply keep your power level at a constant number.

And the best part is: this predictor is accurate across all distances. So if you run 3 kilometers as fast as possible once, you get a very accurate picture of what's possible for a 10 kilometer race, half marathon, or full marathon.

For example, if you look at your wattage instead of your pace, you'll also know exactly how much slower you would have to run against a wind or uphill. Better yet, even downhill, you can see exactly at what level of power you should run to keep your wattage at the right intensity.

Power allows you to clearly see your progress, regardless of whether you primarily run on a running track or in a forest or on a hill.

Sure, this all sounds good. But doesn't heart rate measure your progression and the capability of your body too?

1.2 What works for you: training by power, heart rate or pace?

Many runners who take their sport seriously have a heart rate monitor. They know their heart rate zones, and they know how they perform best. This allows them to train and measure their progression in a targeted manner.

Why is heart rate monitoring so popular with runners?

In 1982, Polar was the first company to come up with a watch for a wide audience that could measure heart rate. With smartphones, Fitbits, heart rate monitors, pedometers, and the Apple Watch, we now have endless brands and devices with which we can measure heart rate, steps, speed, sleep, activity, and stress. But in the early eighties, Polar was actually the first to launch a watch with which you could collect data from your own body. And the data you could collect was heart rate. With a strap around your chest and a watch connected to it, you could see what your heart rate was while you were running.

Many researchers and exercise physiologists used these devices to conduct research on topics such as the relationship between heart rate and fuel consumption. We learned that at a low heart rate you use your fats relatively more, and that at higher heart rates you use your glycogen stores more (for an explanation of glycogen, see the in-depth text in blue font). The relationship between heart rate and lactic acid was extensively explored, and the tipping point became a value that, as an avid runner, you simply had to know. The tipping point (or anaerobic threshold, AT point) is the heart rate at which you produce more lactic acid than your body can process. Lactic acid is sometimes mistakenly seen only as a waste product. What not everyone knows, is that you also produce lactic acid with light exertion, and that in low doses, lactic acid is used by the heart as fuel. It's only when you produce more lactic acid than you can use, that it starts to become an issue. As lactic acid accumulates, you start affecting your performance, and you use your glycogen stores to the fullest. You can maintain this intensity for about an hour.

ANAEROBIC THRESHOLD AND FUEL

Is the anaerobic threshold a new concept for you? We'll briefly explain what it is and why it's so valuable for a runner to know about it. If you exercise more intensively, your muscles need more oxygen because energy must be released faster. That's why your heart rate goes up with physical exertion: your heart pumps more oxygen to your muscles. If you accelerate after a gentle warm up, your heart rate will increase, as will your breathing frequency and tidal volume. In the beginning you will breathe deeper, but not faster. There will automatically come a point (if you keep increasing intensity) at which you can no longer breathe deeper, but your thighs do require more oxygen. That's when you start to breathe faster. This is the moment when the training stimulus starts. At your aerobic threshold, and above this effort, you will build up fitness. It's called the aerobic threshold because when you're taking in a lot of oxygen, you can mainly use your fats as fuel. You can maintain this intensity for between four to six hours. If you keep increasing intensity beyond the aerobic threshold, you will reach your anaerobic threshold. You breathe less deeply and exponentially faster, lactic acid accumulates, and you can maintain this effort for about an hour while mainly burning glycogen. You have four fuels to draw from: ATP, Creatine Phosphate, Glycogen, and Fat. Glycogen and fat are particularly important for endurance athletes. You can run quite a few marathons with your fats as fuel. The big advantage of fat is that you can take a lot of energy with you, even if you have a relatively low weight. Even if you have a fat percentage of 8% (which is very low) and you weigh 70 kilos (154 lbs), you still have 5.6 kilos (12.3 lbs) of fat, good for more than six marathons. A disadvantage of fat is that it does provide energy, but the energy is released slowly. A lot of oxygen is needed, and you don't get the energy directly. So if you run slowly, you can use your fats, but if you increase intensity, you also need another fuel: your glycogen. You have about 500 grams (1.1 lbs) of your glycogen stored in your muscles and in your liver. These 500 grams equal approximately 2000 kCal.

Every runner has enough fat to live on for weeks. We sometimes joke that you can easily find out exactly for how long you can persist with fuel stored in your fat stores: stop eating, and then wait until you die. That's how long. You can go without food for more than 40 days, which shows that you have fuel that you can really use for a long time. A property of fats is that they

21

are energy efficient and last a long time. When you sit in a chair and you're relaxed, you mainly use your energy-efficient fats. When you go for a run, you also use your energy-fast sugars.

You should not confuse these sugars with the sugars in sweets or sports drinks. It's a general term that includes slower carbohydrates. In exercise physiology, these sugars are called glycogen stores. This glycogen is stored in your liver and around your muscles. A well-trained runner can run on maximum glycogen use for about one and a half to two hours. However, it's not true that the combustion of one fuel stops before the other continues. In other words, you're never running on only fat or only glycogen. And, fat always contributes. As you keep adding intensity, more muscle fibers are involved that "eat" something else. So the idea that one system is switched on (glycogen) and that your other system (fats) no longer participates, is not the case. The fact that oxygen uptake increases proportionally with increasing load provides evidence that both systems remain active. If the "fat burners in your muscles" (which use the most oxygen) stop, the oxygen uptake would no longer increase linearly. Oxygen uptake does increase linearly, showing that fat burning does indeed continue throughout.

Okay. But how is this knowledge useful?
Because you always have more fat than glycogen, as a runner, you want to achieve two things with training:
1. Run as fast as possible on your energy-efficient fats
2. Store as much glycogen as possible in your liver and muscles.

FUN FACT: a kilo (2.2 lbs) of fat is good for 9000 kcal. So, if you weigh 70 kg (154 lbs) and you have a body fat percentage of 20%, you have 14 kilos of fat x 9000 kcal = 126,000 kcal fat. You can store about 500 grams of glycogen, which is about 2000 kcal. With this knowledge, you immediately know why many training plan emphasize that variation is important. You want to train your muscles to run efficiently on fats, and you want to stimulate your muscles to store glycogen.

Many heart rate monitors therefore work with zones based on aerobic and anaerobic tresholds.

There are three main zones:

I.   Very easy, little training effect. It's about recovery. For your body, fuel consumption is comparable to sitting on the couch: not much happens. In terms of training, however, it's a part of your plan that should not be underestimated. In this zone, you run, but you don't build up fatigue or damage your muscles, tendons, ligaments, and joints.

II. If you exercise more intensively, you will reach the aerobic threshold. This is where the training effect begins.

III. If you keep increasing intensity, you will arrive at your lactate acid tipping point, and you will no longer be able to maintain your power. This is the anaerobic threshold.

Though we describe 3 zones here, you will often see 5 zones in heart rate training because 3 zones are distinguished between the aerobic threshold and the anaerobic threshold (low, medium, high) and there is also a separate zone above this tipping point.

Pay attention

You can enter your own heart rate zones when training by heart rate. This way, you'll have (reliable) values that you already know. Even if you don't enter zones, you'll still see different zones from your heart rate monitor. Note: this is unreliable. If you take your new heart rate monitor out of the box and you turn it on, you'll have to answer some questions. What language do you speak? What time is it? Do you want a 12h or 24h time format? Are you male or female? Do you wear your watch on the left or right? How much do you weigh? What's your year of birth? And that's where it goes wrong. Your watch determines your maximum heart rate based on your age. There's a standard formula that determines your maximum heart rate as follows: 220 minus your age. Based on this calculated maximum heart rate, the monitor will determine your zones. This is a shame. Because, for many runners, this standard formula does not apply at all. Suppose, you're 45 years old and you have an actual maximum heart rate of 195 (which is not surprising at all). Your watch says 220 minus your age (45) = a maximum heart rate of 175. If you then train in your zones in a targeted manner, you'll become quite annoyed. Because, every time you run smoothly, your heart rate monitor starts to beep that you should slow down. In this way, you structurally train too carefully, and at a certain point you'll no longer make progress.

That's a shame.

You can do better.

Heart rate measurement has taught us a lot in the last 40 years. And with a reliable heart rate monitor and sufficient knowledge, you can train on flat terrain as long as you don't do short intervals. In some cases, however, a heart rate monitor is not suitable. For example, with your interval training of 200 or 400 meters. By the time your heart rate is high, you're already at the end. Running uphill is another issue when training by heart rate. Your pace drops, your heart rate shoots up, and your results are hard to compare to your flat training laps. But the biggest "danger" of heart rate training is an inaccurately measured heart rate. Many major brands have switched from measurements via a strap around the chest to a wrist monitor, and those are still far from accurate for everyone. Runners who often suffer from cold hands generally get inaccurately low heart rate values from a wrist monitor. Author Ron himself has a different experience. His wrist monitor indicates values that are too high.

If you look at the physiology of a person, it actually makes much more sense to measure breaths, instead of heart rate.

The three stages we mentioned earlier can be registered faster and more clearly by looking at your breathing. When you get up from the couch and go outside to run, you start to breathe deeper. So, the first zone is that you take deeper breaths, without breathing faster. At the aerobic threshold, your thighs ask for more oxygen and you breathe faster, as we described in the box about aerobic threshold. You keep increasing intensity, so you'll breathe faster and faster, with the same tidal volume until you reach your tipping point, the anaerobic threshold. At this point, you can no longer deepen your breathing. Because you still need more oxygen, you'll breathe faster, but more shallowly.

Physiologically, your breathing responds faster than your heart rate, which makes it ideal for targeted training. It's just that, back in 1982, it was easier for the company Polar to measure heart rate via a belt than to measure respiratory frequency and tidal volume, so they decided to go with the heart rate monitor.

Well before heart rate monitors emerged, enthusiastic runners trained by pace.

Funnily enough, training by pace in the 1970s and 1980s was very reliable, but nowadays that's no longer the case. How is that possible? Fifty years ago there were no watches that determined your speed via GPS. So, if you started training focused on pace, you were forced to train with a stopwatch and to know your distance very precisely. On an athletics track you could calculate exactly how fast you had to run your 200, 400 or 1000 meters to train at a certain pace. That way of pace training is of course still reliable and still popular with track workouts. With your fastest time at a certain distance (3, 5 or 10 kilometers,) you can calculate what your possible times are at other distances, and you can also determine what your intensive interval paces or your leisurely endurance runs are.

So, what's the problem?

Many runners have a Garmin, Polar, Suunto, or Coros and train by pace using their watch as a compass. Unfortunately, this way of measuring is not always reliable because the watch bases your speed on GPS data. Your watch is connected to satellites and uses the distance between the different position measuring points to know how fast you took to go from point A to point B. Tall buildings, trees with wet leaves, winding roads, or not enough connected satellites can all contribute to GPS measurement errors. Pace based on GPS varies from moment to moment and is not very useful. Of course, the measurements are more stable over longer distances because deviations average out. Therefore, if you run a marathon, your distance will always be around 42.195 km (26.2 miles), although you're not always running the ideal line and your watch is always slightly off. We all know that when training on a track and using Strava it sometimes seems as if you have cut straight across the middle area. That's simply because your watch combined two "satellite" points and missed the curve in between.

Another disadvantage of running with a heart rate monitor is that your heart rate responds slowly. When you run up a hill, your muscles immediately use more energy, but your heart rate takes time to notice that your muscles need more oxygen and it needs to pump faster. So, if you run up a hill with a constant heart rate, you have to work hard for the first part and you have to run very slowly for the second part.

That is one of the great advantages of training with Stryd. You train by power and Stryd does not depend on GPS or heart rate, but measures your power with accelerometers on your foot. And that turns out to be extremely reliable. The breakthrough in power running came with the use of inertial measurement units (IMUs). We prefer to call them accelerometers. These are small instruments in a chip that can be used to measure accelerations. The measuring principle is based on the fact that the crystals in the chip produce a piezoelectric effect under the influence of an acceleration. This piezoelectric effect results in a voltage that can be measured. The Stryd chip accurately measures this voltage much more than 100 times per second, which makes the device ingenious and reliable.

"Ehhhh, Ron and Hans, I really don't know what you're saying now. Plain human language please. "

* Laughter * "Okay, we have a great every day example."

Thanks to an accelerometer, your mobile phone knows whether you are holding it horizontally or vertically. If you watch a video on YouTube and you tilt your phone, the image on your screen will tilt. With the same type of technology, your running watch knows your cadence and the number of steps. Accelerometers today are very cheap, very accurate, and they are found in all kinds of devices, such as smartphones, cars, tablets, pedometers and running watches. A smart power meter uses this technology to determine your speed and stride cadence. And that turns out to be much more reliable than GPS. The Stryd power meter is currently leading the way in converting this technology into reliable speed (and power) measurements for runners.

The sensor includes a number of accelerometers. These measure the acceleration of your body while running in 3 directions: horizontal, vertical, and lateral/sideways. Obviously, in running, it's important to limit vertical and lateral movements, as this consumes energy that doesn't contribute to forward displacement. Everyone has a certain optimal economic step frequency and technique. With Stryd you can determine which running technique suits you best.

As mentioned, Stryd takes measurements many times per second, which makes the accuracy of the device very precise. And Stryd doesn't just measure your movement from side to side, top to bottom, and your speed forward, but also air pressure, temperature, and humidity.

These measurements, combined with your weight and height, together with Stryd's well thought-out algorithms, accurately reflect your power. When you run, you can see your power (in Watts) via your smartphone, your Apple Watch or your running watch. Power (P) is calculated from your weight (m) (in kg), the measured acceleration (a) (in m/s^2, in 3 directions), the speed (v) (in m/s), and the air resistance with the basic formulas:

$$F = m * a$$
$$P = F * v$$

Stryd's breakthrough is the software it has developed to calculate the power by using all data from the accelerometers continuously and in real time. As we saw, the basic formulas are simple but a complicated algorithm is needed to accurately calculate the power based on the accelerations in all directions.

The advantage of the Stryd foot pod is that it gives you a pure and exact measurement of power in real time. This gives a much better and objective picture of your effort than your feeling, your speed, or your heart rate alone.

And the biggest advantage for runners who prefer simplicity, rather than to read complicated books about training: you only need to train with 1 number in mind. As long as you know which level of power you need for which training, that's enough.

Why the wattages from Polar and Garmin are wrong.

One of Koen's running friends wanted to know what his expected time was on the half marathon. To calculate, he used the power of a fast 10K.

"I may not have gone all the way because I was running alone, but I did my best anyway," said Joost.

His time on the 10 kilometer was 44:15 and his power was 357 Watts. So, Koen and Joost used 357 Watts as his Critical Power and started calculating.

According to the formulas, after some calculations, Joost would end up with a half marathon of 1:16:34 ". That can't be true, said Koen.

"Did you enter your correct weight in Stryd?"

"I don't have Stryd," said Joost. "I measured it with my Polar."

What did we find out? The power measured by Polar (and Garmin) is far too high. Hans and Ron have done several studies that showed that the wattages of Polar and were about 25% higher than those of Stryd. The differences can be explained by the fact that Polar and Garmin developed their power readings from measurements with force plates in the lab. However, this doesn't take into account the energy recovery in the muscles during the landing phase. Stryd bases calculations on the actual power required to move around while running, resulting in this difference of 25%. In addition, Polar and Garmin use GPS, which is much less accurate. Incidentally, the relatively new brand Coros does make use of the necessary power to move around while running. Coros has fully integrated the information from the Stryd foot pod. This makes the Coros watch a strong duo with Stryd. Coros can also measure power based on GPS, but this is less accurate, especially with changes in speed and course. Coros also doesn't take into account the resistance from the wind. So for now, Stryd works best.

1.3 What is Critical Power and what can you do with it?

In the previous chapter, we wrote about the tipping point (anaerobic threshold) and different heart rate zones. When running by power, your Critical Power (CP) is a valuable number to know. You can use it to determine your different training zones.

Your Critical Power is the power that you can maintain for a certain duration. Because of this definition, it can sometimes be confusing. In sports literature, this could be the power that you can sustain for 20 minutes (CP20), 45 minutes (CP45), or 60 minutes (CP60). CP60 is lower in wattage than CP45. And CP45 is lower than CP20. After all, you can last for a shorter time with a higher power.

Stryd uses one Critical Power, calculated based on your power curve. Without knowing your Critical Power you can't properly use your power for training and races. A power of, for example, 260 Watts says nothing, just like a heart rate of, for example, 173 doesn't say anything.

For the information you gather to be useful, you need to know what power you can maintain for a certain period of time.

Until recently, you had to do an exercise test with a sports doctor to accurately determine your heart rate zones. On a bicycle or a treadmill you would go through increasing levels of cycling or running harder and faster. A sports doctor would take a small sample of your blood at each level to measure your lactic acid values, or you would have to wear a mask for a breath analysis. A major disadvantage of these expensive tests was that athletes regularly got anxious from wearing the mask or doing the blood test, and that the measurements were therefore not completely true to reality in comparison with outdoor sports. For example, it was possible that (due to rapid breathing) the anaerobic threshold was set too low and athletes started exercising with heart rate levels that were lower than they should be. Result: frustration due to slow pace and little progression because of overly cautious training.

A power meter has the great advantage that you can determine your Critical Power outside on the street or in nature.

You can take a test to determine your Critical Power, but Stryd also has a feature to automatically adjust your Critical Power based on your workouts: auto-calculated Critical Power. Basically, Stryd itself determines your Critical Power based on a series of training sessions and races. The auto-calculated Critical Power is accurate to 1 - 2% for most runners, and adjusts automatically as runners get fitter or out of shape.

You get a good indication of your Critical Power when you first start, 3 training sessions with sufficient variation are required.

For example:
1. Short distance, sprints or accelerations with a duration of 10 to 30 seconds;
2. Medium distance, a 10 to 20 minute pace run, or a 5 km or 10 km at your race pace.
3. Long distance, a gentle endurance run of at least 50 minutes.

After that, the workouts are tracked for the last 90 days and your Critical Power becomes increasingly more accurate.

Every workout counts.

The fact that every run is automatically included in your Critical Power is a luxury that will give you enormous benefits in the long term. In the past you probably went to a sports doctor once a year to determine your VO_2 max and your heart rate zones. With Stryd, every training is analyzed and compared with your values from the past. As with any new device, it takes a little thought and dedication to download Stryd's app and pair your Stryd with your phone and watch. But once you've done that, you'll have the smartest and most loyal trainer in the world, sitting right on top of your shoe. In the app you will see various data under Summary: Stress, Running Stress Balance, Upcoming Events, Power Duration Curve, and Critical Power at the bottom. First, you'll see your power (in orange), and then your power per kilogram of body weight.

You'll only want to know one thing: that your power per kilogram of body weight is as high as possible.

It can be very addictive (in a good way!) to work to increase your Critical Power. We see regular sessions on Strava with the subject: Critical Power boost workout. After your workout you'll have to wait anxiously to see if you've earned the notification: 'Your Critical Power has increased!'

Warning: make sure you always train with Stryd. Koen was once notified that his Critical Power had increased to 5.26 Watts/kg. That would allow Koen to run a marathon within 2.5 hours and that's not feasible. What had happened? Koen was running with different running shoes and had forgotten to put his Stryd on his new shoes. So the readings were coming from his Polar Vantage V, not Stryd, and were inaccurately high. Due to the link between Stryd, Strava, and Polar, the training was stored in Stryd's PowerCenter and included in Koen's calculations. You can easily ensure that Stryd doesn't include one of your sessions in your results. Go to the app and click on Calendar. Click on your training and at the top right you see three horizontal dots. Click on view details and voilà: your training. Include Run in Analysis is normally green. Slide the ball to gray and your training will not be taken into account.

You see: it's not complicated, but it is more convenient to just train with your Stryd, then you won't have this problem at all.

If your Critical Power suddenly drops a number of points, it means that your Critical Power was determined more than 90 days ago and that you haven't trained at the level of your Critical Power for 90 days. In short, did your Critical Power drop? Then it's time to get to work!

Sounds good, but what exactly does your Critical Power do for you?

If you're stuck at the same level at the moment but would like to improve your PB on the 5K, 10K, half marathon or full marathon, then your Critical Power is priceless.

Variation in training is important, especially if you train specifically for a PB. Five zones emerge from your personal Critical Power:

Easy

Moderate

Threshold (upper limit of Threshold is your Critical Power)

Interval

Repetition

In the chapters focusing on the different distances (5K, 10K, half marathon, and full marathon), we'll discuss these zones in more detail.

What distinguishes running by power from running by heart rate, is the possibility to do more targeted interval training. The great thing about running by power is that you can work with two zones above your tipping point. You can, of course, run an interval of 200 meters at higher power than intervals of 400 or 600 meters. That distinction can't be made with a heart rate monitor. Above your anaerobic threshold you have only one zone: from your anaerobic threshold to your maximum heart rate. It wouldn't make any sense to have other zones above your anaerobic threshold for short intervals. Just think about it. If you really run 200 meters intensively, it's not hard to overshoot your target. But by the time your heart rate is too high, you've already finished your 200 meters. If you train by power, you can do targeted intervals at 200 meters. For example, if you want to run 320 Watts for 200 meters, you can check after 30 meters (or earlier) whether you're running fast enough (or too fast) and then you can speed up or slow down. Another advantage of power training is that you can go full out any time you want. Of course this is always possible, but normally you don't know exactly how fast you can run at any given distance or time. If you know that you can run 10 kilometers in 50 minutes, it's easy to figure out how fast you would be on a 5K, half marathon, or full marathon. But if your favorite run has a nice segment of (for example) 1380 meters, calculations become a lot more complicated. Doing the math for one segment of a run is manageable, but if you have different segments on different laps where you'd like to go full throttle, you obviously don't want to calculate the ideal time for all those odd distances. For example, for 2130 meters, the ideal run time is slightly different from (for example) 1380 meters. With power and Stryd, all these distances become easy to work with.

What does this have to do with Critical Power?

Based on your Critical Power, you get a beautiful curve showing all wattages between 10 seconds and roughly 3 or more hours. So every distance (and time) is included. And the best part is: you don't have to do any complicated enkelvoud calculation, it's all automatic. So, if you accelerate during (for example) 1380 meters, that's a reliable test run to see whether you're progressing or not. In the Power Duration Curve you see a white line (your potential) and blue segments (your actual results from the past thirty days).

POWER DURATION CURVE

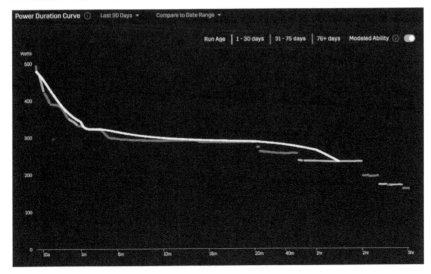

Figure 3: Power Duration Curve

Power Duration Curve

This power curve is very interesting for several reasons.

The power curve is based on your best running performance over the past 90 days.

The power curve can be found in your PowerCenter at Stryd.com. To our know-ledge, there are currently no other parties that work with a power curve for running, although it has long been commonplace in the cycling world. That's why triathletes are so excited about running with power. They're already familiar with the many benefits of the power curve.

What's the benefit of the power curve?

1. You can go full throttle on your favorite segment of your running route and you will always get valuable information from it. So even if it's a hill of 272 meters or a lap with a distance that you don't normally run in a race, like (for example) 5752 meters.

2. You can see at what level of power you have to run for a PB at your favorite distance, and you can quickly see whether that's already feasible or if you still need more training.

We dare to say that your power curve alone is already enough to make meaningful use of a power meter and to train for your PB in a targeted way. Achievements older than 90 days are not included in the curve. It's about what you can do now, not what you were able to do in the past. If you performed well today, the corresponding point in the curve (duration and average power) will improve immediately. If a 90-day performance falls outside the curve, that affects the curve. The next best performance of the past 90 days will take its place.

You can also use the curve the other way around. For example, if you think that 45 minutes on a 10K is feasible, you can check the curve to see which power is associated with that time. Whether or not a certain time is achievable with your current level, can easily be determined using the Race Power Calculator. More on this later.

The Race Power Calculator will give you a good indication of the power level that you must maintain for optimal performance.

1.4 Disadvantages of training by power

We've discussed some of the great benefits of running by power: you don't need a relatively unreliable GPS, and your power responds much faster than heart rate. And even with headwind and uphill terrain you can continue to run by power. Power training provides peace of mind and you can train specifically for a PB.

Are there any disadvantages to training by power?

We often hear from runners who are used to training with a heart rate monitor that the monitor can be a welcome indicator for people with a lot of stress. After all, stress at work or after an illness makes your heart rate go up, so if you train on heart rate, you should naturally run more slowly in times of stress. Also, for avid runners who overtrain, the heart rate monitor can be a remedy if the heart rate no longer rises during intensive training.

Does this happen with running by power?

No. Stryd's power meter determines your Critical Power based on your workouts. Workouts older than 90 days doesn't count towards your Critical Power. That is to say: progress is directly included in your new values, but illness or overtraining is only compensated after 90 days.

Example.

Imagine you run a very fast 10 kilometers in March. You participate in an event and you give it everything you've got. You cross the line exhausted. Red faced. Heavy legs. Nice PB. The following week is rough. Your partner wants to leave you and a colleague is sick, so you're working twice as hard. You just had a hernia surgery. Life is full of heartbreak and stress. If you keep running and only train with Stryd, things can go wrong. Running is a welcome distraction, but your body does not recover as well as you're used to during this difficult period. If you continue to train on your abilities and you train just as often as before all the setbacks, then things are bound to go wrong. After all, your Stryd will take your top time from March into your Critical Power and your zones for another 90 days. The fact that you are gradually performing less is only taken into account in June (90 days after March).

Incidentally, Stryd does monitor your training sessions to check whether you are training constructively, or whether you may be doing unnoticed damage. Stryd indicates this by means of the Running Stress Balance.

What's your Running Stress Balance?

A handy trick from Stryd that we will discuss here is your Running Stress Balance (RSB). Your RSB indicates the difference between your activities of the last 7 days versus the 42 days before. This way, you can see in 1 number whether you're improving, or whether you could use some rest. If your RSB is -40 or lower, it's good to take a few rest days. If you're between -25 and -40, you should be careful. Extra rest works better than an intensive workout. You're training constructively when you're between -10 and -25. It's good to be in between these two points during training periods, and to take some rest days before a race. Between -10 and 5 you'll maintain the condition you have, so if you're training and want to get better, you should put on your running shoes more often (or run more intensively). If you have consciously taken some rest because an important event is coming up, this is fine. Because between 5 and 25 is the perfect RSB to be at, at the start of your event where you want to run a PB (after a training period between -10 and -25). If you're between 25 and 45, then you need a push to get off the couch and start running again. However, this Running Stress Balance is only related to your training, and doesn't know when you're feeling ill or stressed. So, that remains a pitfall of running by power.

This disadvantage of running by power is easy to fix. You can train by power and heart rate. Power controls your training. When training, you only have to pay attention to your power, but in Stryd's PowerCenter or on Strava (or another app where you analyze your workouts) you can check whether your heart rate is keeping up. When you are in good shape, your heart rate will drop over time at a certain wattage. Your body has become stronger (and your Critical Power improved). You deliver more power at fewer revs (heart beats).

Hans and Ron go so far as to keep all data of all training sessions for themselves in Excel. Such information is very educational and will help you avoid unpleasant surprises.

Resting heart rate

Another way to check whether you are recovering sufficiently from your workouts is your resting heart rate. Your resting heart rate is a value that you can measure on a daily basis. It's the heartbeat you have when you sit quietly on the couch. Whether you measure resting heart rate in the morning or in the evening doesn't matter, as long as you do it at the same time. Make sure that you sit for at least 5 minutes, because your heart rate increases just from standing. In any case, it's very educational to measure your resting heart rate for a period of time. You'll gain insight into your recovery in relation to work, sleep, alcohol, jet lag, and training. Is your heart rate five beats higher than you're used to? Then it's time to rest (even if you actually had an intensive interval in mind).

HEART RATE VARIABILITY

More and more heart rate monitors are also showing heart rate variability. That's even more reliable than your resting heart rate. Your heart rate variability is the time difference between two consecutive heartbeats. Are you training in a constructive way and are you recovering well? Then your heart rate variability increases. Contrary to popular belief, it's unhealthy if your heart beats evenly. During your inhalation, your heart rate increases a little and, when you exhale, your heart rate decreases. This is related to two different systems in your autonomic nervous system: your orthosympathetic system and your parasympathetic system. Your orthosympathetic system is your so-called accelerator and stands for action, high heart rate, the upper number of your blood pressure, and rapid breathing. Your parasympathetic system is the recovery, the brake pedal of your body. Your parasympathetic system stands for rest, recovery, low heart rate, the lower number of your blood pressure, and calm relaxed breathing. In times of stress and a lot of work or training, your orthosympathetic system can take the upper hand and even remain active in your sleep. By measuring your heart rate variability, you can keep an eye on this and you can build in rest and take more time for relaxation exercises when needed.

Feeling

We love measuring and making progress transparent. But of course, there are also ways of knowing if you're making progress without using measurements. If you feel fit and full of energy, you're fine. Do you dread your workouts and feel tired and lethargic? Then it is time to rest and listen to your body. Tip: do run, even if you are tired and lethargic. After fifteen minutes of running you'll know whether it's okay to go back home, or whether it's better to keep running to get more energy. Do you still feel tired after running for 15 minutes? Then it's time to rest. But it may well be that you're surprisingly more ready after fifteen minutes of running than when you just stepped out of the door. Then it's fine to finish your workout.

Summarizing, the disadvantage of running by power is that you can't measure fatigue in your body with a power meter.

But, power meters are great for measuring progress. That's why we'll now go to Part II: How can you run faster?

In summary

Power is the amount of energy per second that is required to propel your body in a certain direction at a certain speed.
GPS is not reliable over short distances.

Air resistance is also important for your performance. Air resistance depends on, among other things, temperature, wind speed, air pressure, and height above sea level.
Your Critical Power can be used as a surrogate near your tipping point, or anaerobic threshold.
Every training is included, so your Critical Power automatically remains accurate.
With the Power Duration Curve you have insight into what you can do at specific distances.

Koen de Jong

How can you run faster?

2.1 Weight (mass) and speed: what you need to know

If you want to make progress and sharpen your PB at your favorite distance, introducing variation in your training is important. Are you a runner who often runs the same distance at the same pace? Introducing variation in your training will make a big difference. More on that later.

First, we want to talk about weight. If you're starting a few pounds overweight, losing that extra weight is the fastest way to progress. If you are (for example) twenty pounds heavier than is healthy for your height, you can, of course, train for a PB focused on power. That works, but it's a bit like buying a new house because your windows are dirty. It works, but there's an easier way. Note that we will use mass extensively in the next section rather than weight, but, assuming you are running on earth and not with some other planet's gravity, which term we use does not matter much.

In The Secret of Running Hans and Ron write extensively about the relationship between weight and speed. They've devoted an entire chapter to it: How Much Faster Will You Go When You Lose Weight?

How big is the effect of your mass?

The mathematics of mass impact can be explained simply, according to Hans and Ron. Your body basically has a fixed power, P, in Watts. If you run on a flat course, you use that power to overcome running resistance and air resistance. If you lose a few pounds, your power remains constant (because your strength is unchanged), but your running resistance decreases. Result: you can run faster. There is, however, a limit. Things go wrong at the point where you no longer lose excess fat, but muscle mass. We want to prevent runners to cross the line in their drive to lose weight. The moment your sweat starts to smell like ammonia, it's important to start eating more. But again, knowing you can lose some of

ACHIEVABLE TIMES BY DISTANCE BASED ON CP60 AND VO₂ MAX

CP60			ACHIEVABLE RESULT				VO₂ MAX
Watts/kg	3,000 m	5,000 m	10,000 m	21.1 km	42.195 km	Distance for one hour	ml/kg/min
2.00	0:23:16	0:40:12	1:24:24	3:07:38	6:33:51	7.27	28.0
2.25	0:20:36	0:35:34	1:14:41	2:46:02	5:48:32	8.15	31.5
2.50	0:18:27	0:31:53	1:06:55	2:28:47	5:12:19	9.03	35.0
2.75	0:16:43	0:28:53	1:00:39	2:14:50	4:43:03	9.90	38.5
3.00	0:15:14	0:26:19	0:55:15	2:02:51	4:17:53	10.80	42.0
3.25	0:14:05	0:24:20	0:51:06	1:53:36	3:58:27	11.62	45.5
3.50	0:13:04	0:22:34	0:47:23	1:45:20	3:41:06	12.47	49.0
3.75	0:12:12	0:21:04	0:44:13	1:38:19	3:26:23	13.30	52.4
4.00	0:11:26	0:19:45	0:41:27	1:32:09	3:13:26	14.13	55.9
4.25	0:10:46	0:18:35	0:39:01	1:26:45	3:02:06	14.95	59.4
4.50	0:10:10	0:17:34	0:36:53	1:21:59	2:52:06	15.76	62.9
4.75	0:09:39	0:16:40	0:34:58	1:17:45	2:43:13	16.56	66.4
5.00	0:09:11	0:15:52	0:33:18	1:14:01	2:35:23	17.34	69.9
5.25	0:08:46	0:15:08	0:31:46	1:10:37	2:28:14	18.12	73.4
5.50	0:08:23	0:14:29	0:30:24	1:07:35	2:21:52	18.88	76.9
5.75	0:08:02	0:13:53	0:29:08	1:04:47	2:16:00	19.64	80.4
6.00	0:07:43	0:13:20	0:28:01	1:02:16	2:10:43	20.38	83.9
6.25	0:07:26	0:12:51	0:26:58	0:59:56	2:05:49	21.12	87.4
6.50	0:07:10	0:12:23	0:26:01	0:57:50	2:02:23	21.84	90.9

Figure 4: What times are achievable?

your extra pounds is an easy way to boost your speed. Overall, you can say that for every excess percent that you become lighter, you also become one percent faster. This makes sense, because you use less energy when you are lighter, while your heart-lung system is unchanged. Note: this is a simplified explanation. It does not take into account certain physiological complexities, but generally applies to situations where excess weight is being lost.

For this reason, your Critical Power (just like your thresholds) only becomes interesting when you start looking at your power per kilogram of body mass. So, a Critical Power of 250 Watts doesn't say anything about your possible run times. If your mass is 60 kilos (a weight of 132 lbs), your power per kilogram of body mass is 4.1, but at a mass of 80 kilos (a weight of 178 lbs), your power per kilogram body mass is 3.1. For example, a 10 kilometer run with a Critical Power of 4.1 Watts per kilogram of body mass takes around 41 minutes. The same run with a power of 3.1 Watts per kilogram of body weight takes around 54 minutes. So, your power per kilogram of body weight is what matters, not your absolute power.

PERFORMANCE COMPARISON FOR MALES

Classification	CP60 Watts/kg 30 years	CP60 Watts/kg 40 years	CP60 Watts/kg 50 years	CP60 Watts/kg 60 years	CP60 Watts/kg 70 years	CP60 Watts/kg 80 years
Absolute top	6.4	6.0	5.6	5.2	4.7	4.0
International	5.7	5.4	5.1	4.7	4.2	3.6
National	5.1	4.8	4.5	4.2	3.8	3.2
Regional	4.5	4.2	3.9	3.6	3.3	2.8
Running Enthusiast	3.8	3.6	3.4	3.1	2.8	2.4
Fitness Runner	3.2	3.0	2.8	2.6	2.4	2.0
Untrained	2.5	2.4	2.2	2.1	1.9	1.6
Poor	1.9	1.8	1.7	1.6	1.4	1.2
Very Poor	1.3	1.2	1.1	1.0	0.9	0.8

Figure 5: Performance Comparison for Males by Age

PERFORMANCE COMPARISON FOR FEMALES

Classification	CP60 Watts/kg 30 years	CP60 Watts/kg 40 years	CP60 Watts/kg 50 years	CP60 Watts/kg 60 years	CP60 Watts/kg 70 years	CP60 Watts/kg 80 years
Absolute top	5.7	5.4	5.0	4.6	4.2	3.6
International	5.1	4.8	4.5	4.2	3.7	3.2
National	4.6	4.3	4.0	3.7	3.3	2.9
Regional	4.0	3.8	3.5	3.2	2.9	2.5
Running Enthusiast	3.4	3.2	3.0	2.8	2.5	2.2
Fitness Runner	2.9	2.7	2.5	2.3	2.1	1.8
Untrained	2.3	2.1	2.0	1.8	1.7	1.4
Poor	1.7	1.6	1.5	1.4	1.2	1.1
Very Poor	1.1	1.1	1.0	0.9	0.8	0.7

Figure 5: Performance Comparison for Females by Age

In the table in image 4 you can see your favorite distance and your potential times at your current Watts/kg.

If the numbers start to make you dizzy, don't panic. For runners who already run with Stryd, the Critical Power per kg isn't rocket science. After all, you can easily go to your settings in the app and look at your Critical Power. You will then automatically see your power in Watts/kg. If this book is your first introduction to running with power, then you should remember: if you lose 1% excess weight, you will run 1% faster.

Not just theory

The above statements and figures have not only been studied theoretically, but have also been proven in practice in people who have lost excess weight. For example, Hans weighed 127 pounds in 1980 (with a height of 5'7"). More than thirty years later, he'd gained twenty pounds. With a targeted diet, Hans returned to his old weight of 57.5 kg (127 pound) in six months, a decrease of 15% in weight. His performance at all distances increased spectacularly during that period. In the end - you guessed it - Hans became 15% (!) faster on all distances. Note: This is a personal anecdote; the effort to lose weight and the cost of losing too much weight vary across sex and age - please consult your doctor if you are not sure about your personal case!

Important: All of these situations only apply when someone has extra weight to lose. It can be dangerous to restrict your eating too much to hit a given weight. In this chapter, we're referring to runners who have a few pounds more than they should - not runners who are already at a healthy weight.

In addition to weight/mass, age also influences your running times. For example, if your Critical Power is 3.8 Watts/kg, it makes a big difference in races whether you are 32 years old or 72 years old. As a 32-year-old, a Critical Power of 3.8 Watts/kg is an excellent value, but you won't find yourself at the top of performers for your age. However, if you're 72 years old and are still running at 3.8 Watts/kg, you will find yourself alongside the very best in your age.
Hans and Ron made a nice overview of the levels per age category for women and men.

2.2 Train in your zones

Where are you?

Earlier, we wrote about 5 different zones. We'll discuss this in more detail in this chapter. Some watches work with D0, D1, D2, D3 and AT+, with AT corresponding to your Critical Power or anaerobic threshold. Other watches keep zones Z1, Z2, Z3, Z4 and Z5. Stryd also works with 5 zones: Easy, Moderate, Threshold, Interval, and Repetition..

The zones are similar, but not completely interchangeable. For example, Stryd works with two zones above Critical Power, while heart rate watches only have one zone after the anaerobic threshold.

How do you use the zones in your training?

Variation is the magic word if you want to make progress. The main reason why you want to know your different zones is because of the two fuels you carry with you: fats and sugars (glycogen). We've already described the different fuels in detail earlier. As you know, as an endurance athlete, you mainly use fats and glycogen. You use your fat stores when you run slowly, and glycogen becomes your main fuel when you run faster. Variation in training between your fuels makes you faster and provides a good basis to work from.

Variation is needed to use your fats efficiently as fuel and to maximize your glycogen stores. You need a good mix between gentle training and intensive stimuli, combined with good recovery.

After all, you don't get better during training, but during the recovery afterwards.

You can teach your body to run faster on your fats, partly by running slow and long. Note: this is your Zone 1 (or D0) on a heart rate monitor, and the Easy zone in Stryd.

This zone is variable in running intensity. If you make progress, you can run faster on your fats and thus your pace will increase. You see this when you train with heart rate: you run faster at the same heart rate. This is fully reflected when you run by power: your powers in this lowest zone go up.

Gentle workouts are good for the basics. If you train more intensively, you will enter an important zone where your body can choose which fuel to use: fats or glycogen. This zone lasts from Easy to Critical Power.

Which fuel your body prefers in this zone depends, among other things, on stress and nutrition. Do you have a lot of stress and do you eat a lot of sugar and carbohydrates? Then your body prefers glycogen combustion. In addition to stress and nutrition, your workout is of course also a trigger for fat or glycogen burning.

Above Critical Power, you mainly burn your glycogen while your fat burning plays a smaller part. With Stryd, the two zones between Easy and Critical Power are called Moderate and Threshold. The slower you run, the more your body can rely on your fat stores. There's a lot to be gained there with targeted training in the various zones. You get to know your body and you learn which zones you've barely trained at the moment. Especially in the beginning, runners often notice that they have a strong preference for one zone over others.

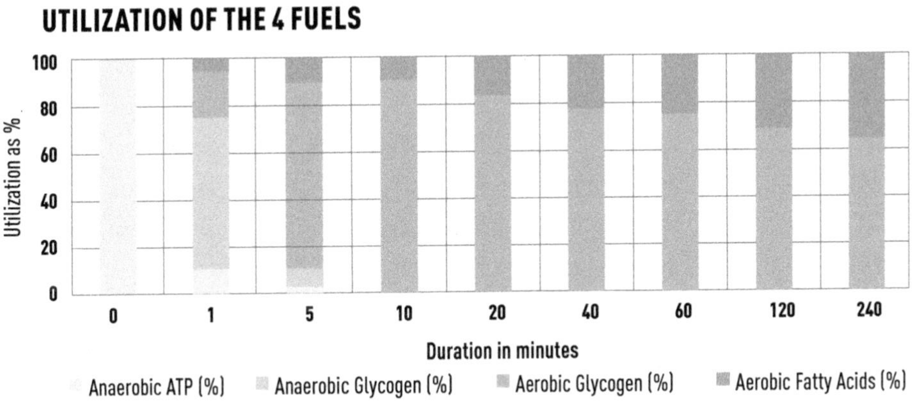

UTILIZATION OF THE 4 FUELS

Figure 6: 4 Energy Systems

So either fast or very calm.

Are you a runner who sees a training session (or would you rather call it a workout?) as a good moment to catch up with a friend? Then there is a good chance that you have a great base in the low zones, but that you have to get used to more intensive training.

Or do you think that training doesn't make sense if you don't sweat a lot and have muscle pain? There's a good chance that you'll improve a lot if you also include slow training sessions. Training at a slow pace is not a waste of time. Actually, it's meaningful training which helps build a solid foundation.

Figure 6 shows which fuel is most useful to you in percentage terms at maximum effort. You can see that, starting from 5 minutes, your glycogen and your fatty acids are the main fuels used. In this figure, we make the assumption that you run as fast as possible. If you run slower, you will use more fatty acids, proportionally. Smart variation in intensity and duration of your workouts ensures that all energy systems are trained. Note: through smart training and healthy nutrition you can train your body to run more efficiently on your fatty acids.

In the chapter What is Critical Power and what can you do with it?, we discussed the Power Duration Curve.

This curve is a great way to check whether you train with enough variation, and whether you're engaging all energy systems during your training sessions.

In the curve in your Stryd app, you can see your maximum power from 10 seconds to roughly 3 hours (depending on how long you run) from the past ninety days. To get a nice, personal graph, it's good to sprint at least once for 10 seconds, preferably also uphill or against the wind. And to run a long endurance run at a good pace. The curve also shows whether you've run this wattage in the past 30 days, whether it was between 31 days and 75 days, or more than 76 days. Anything older than 90 days is not taken into consideration.

How does the curve help to check if you have enough variation in your training?

If the Power Duration Curve is a smooth line for the past ninety days, then you know that you've trained with plenty of variation. However, if you see that your line is discontinuous and drops at certain times, then there is an opportunity for improvement.

In this example you can compare your actual power duration curve with the modeled curve (white), which is an estimate for the power you are capable of at all durations, even if you have not produced power data at all durations. Based on this curve, runners can target specific areas of their curve to improve. For example, they could perform a max effort 3 minute activity and a max effort 20-50 minutes activity, two durations which will help improve the overall accuracy of your Critical Power.

POWER DURATION CURVE

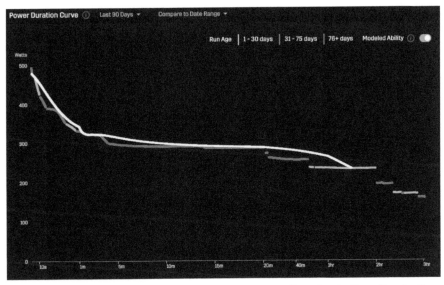

Figure 3 again: Power Duration Curve

2.3 The power of intervals

A solid foundation of base training helps you achieve a higher base speed. If your base is good and you've already trained a lot in your different zones, then intervals are a good way to become even faster. Targeted interval training is simpler and more precise with power, compared to heart rate interval training.

By training with intervals you can train at a high intensity. This improves your base speed and your body gets used to excess lactic acid. Because of the rest in between the intervals, these types of workouts are not as stressful as a race, and you can do this kind of training more often. Depending on the goal, the length of the intervals and the intermediate rest varies from one training plan to another. The intensity with which you run intervals also varies. Some intervals are almost full speed, other intervals you go fast, but still somewhat with the brakes on.

How do you know which pace and which distance is most suitable for your intervals?

INTERVAL DISTANCE	PERCENTAGE OF CP60
[m]	[%]
2000	100%
1600	102%
1200	104%
1000	107%
800	109%
600	114%
400	120%
200	126%
100	133%

Figure 7: Power Target for Interval Training

Books have been written about the ideal distances and paces for intervals. It's a delicate job to determine exactly which pace is most suitable for your 200 meters, your 400 meters, your 600 meters, etc. If you've already calculated at what pace (your heart rate monitor will not help you on short distances anyway) you have to run a

200 meter distance, it will still take you several weeks (or months) before you know exactly what is the best pace for you. As described earlier, your GPS is also not very useful during targeted, short intervals.

However, with Stryd it becomes really easy to do your intervals. Because Stryd immediately measures what you're doing, you can check after 10 meters on a 200 meter sprint whether you are on track or not. Because - we repeat - power is the amount of energy per second that your body needs to push your mass in the given direction. This applies to a marathon, a half marathon, but also for a 400 meter or 200 meter interval.

And now it gets interesting for runners who want to run faster and are willing to train hard in a targeted manner.

In the table you can see at what percentage of your CP60 you should target for specific intervals.

So, for example, if your CP60 is 257 Watts, then your ideal power for an interval of 400 meters is 308 Watts (257 * 120%).

The fact that you see the percentages increase considerably at short interval distances is because your anaerobic energy systems supply extra energy there. Your anaerobic fuel supply is limited. You will benefit from a 100 meter or a 200 meter interval, but this benefit is lost at 1000 meters.

Experience. In 2019 I (KdJ) trained for the Amsterdam marathon. Since I really wanted to run the marathon in sub 3 hours, I left nothing to chance. So, I started to pay attention to my technique, I lost some weight, and I started training my intervals more specifically. After some calculations and consultation, I had determined my ideal pace for 400 meters. After that, it took a few weeks before I could run my 400 meters in 87 seconds. I was used to running by heart rate and had never done interval training before. It took some time getting used to. When I started running with Stryd, one of the first things I tested was interval training. According to Stryd, I was able to run 308 Watts during my 400 meter intervals. After a warm up, I walked to the starting line of the athletics track and started at a brisk pace. Still in the first bend, I couldn't resist checking my watch to see what power I was running: 308 Watts?! For the entire 400 meters my power fluctuated between 305 and 311 Watts and I was flabbergasted when I saw that I had run exactly 87 seconds. Then I started training using 200 meter (323 Watts) and 1000 meter (274 Watts) intervals (because I hadn't done those distances before). It was a revelation. The quality of my training improved immensely and it was all very simple. Much easier than figuring out with what pace or heart rate to run.

Do you know if you're already close to your maximum potential, or if there's still a lot of progress to be made at your favorite distance? In the next chapter, we'll look at how Stryd can help you estimate your potential personal bests at the 5K, 10K, Half Marathon, and Full Marathon.

2.4 How fast can you run?

As a runner, it's interesting to know what your potential PB is for a certain distance. Even if a personal best isn't your main reason for running, it's still nice to make progress and know what time you can run for a certain distance. Based on your PB for one distance, 5 kilometers for example, you can find calculation models on the Internet where your attainable times are calculated

ACHIEVABLE TIMES BY DISTANCE BASED ON CP60 AND VO₂ MAX

CP60			ACHIEVABLE RESULT				VO₂ MAX
Watts/kg	3,000 m	5,000 m	10,000 m	21.1 km	42.195 km	Distance for one hour	ml/kg/min
2.00	0:23:16	0:40:12	1:24:24	3:07:38	6:33:51	7.27	28.0
2.25	0:20:36	0:35:34	1:14:41	2:46:02	5:48:32	8.15	31.5
2.50	0:18:27	0:31:53	1:06:55	2:28:47	5:12:19	9.03	35.0
2.75	0:16:43	0:28:53	1:00:39	2:14:50	4:43:03	9.90	38.5
3.00	0:15:14	0:26:19	0:55:15	2:02:51	4:17:53	10.80	42.0
3.25	0:14:05	0:24:20	0:51:06	1:53:36	3:58:27	11.62	45.5
3.50	0:13:04	0:22:34	0:47:23	1:45:20	3:41:06	12.47	49.0
3.75	0:12:12	0:21:04	0:44:13	1:38:19	3:26:23	13.30	52.4
4.00	0:11:26	0:19:45	0:41:27	1:32:09	3:13:26	14.13	55.9
4.25	0:10:46	0:18:35	0:39:01	1:26:45	3:02:06	14.95	59.4
4.50	0:10:10	0:17:34	0:36:53	1:21:59	2:52:06	15.76	62.9
4.75	0:09:39	0:16:40	0:34:58	1:17:45	2:43:13	16.56	66.4
5.00	0:09:11	0:15:52	0:33:18	1:14:01	2:35:23	17.34	69.9
5.25	0:08:46	0:15:08	0:31:46	1:10:37	2:28:14	18.12	73.4
5.50	0:08:23	0:14:29	0:30:24	1:07:35	2:21:52	18.88	76.9
5.75	0:08:02	0:13:53	0:29:08	1:04:47	2:16:00	19.64	80.4
6.00	0:07:43	0:13:20	0:28:01	1:02:16	2:10:43	20.38	83.9
6.25	0:07:26	0:12:51	0:26:58	0:59:56	2:05:49	21.12	87.4
6.50	0:07:10	0:12:23	0:26:01	0:57:50	2:02:23	21.84	90.9

Figure 4 again: What times are achievable?

for other distances. There are reliable calculation models to determine your potential for the 10K, half marathon, and marathon based on your PB for the 5K. However, this is only true if you ran the 5K under ideal conditions (8 degrees Celsius (46 degrees Fahrenheit), hardly any wind, no elevation, and your lowest healthy weight). Then the comparison is only valid while these variables remain the same. In practice, this is almost never the case. Temperature and wind, for example, are highly variable, which makes it difficult to compare one event with another.

Good news for runners with a Stryd power meter: determining your attainable time at different distances is more accurate and easier than ever. Even temperature, elevation, and wind are included.

First, we go back to your Critical Power.

With an accurate Critical Power you can determine which times you can run at different distances. Below, we first take a look at the schedule from Ron and Hans, as we saw earlier in the chapter about weight (mass) and times. In the overview in figure 4, you can see your possible times at 3K, 5K, 10K, 15K, half marathon, and full marathon per Watts/kg. The times naturally take into account a decline at longer distances. You may be relatively better at 5 kilometers, or on longer distances, such as a half or full marathon. Some people notice that the times aren't quite right for them, but the predicted finish times based on your Watts/kg can be a good target time, and for most runners the formula works well.

Although these times are a nice guideline, Ron and Hans can't include everything in this overview. For example: temperature. 8 degrees Celsius (49°F) is an ideal temperature for top runners in a marathon, but what should you do if it's not 8 degrees Celsius (46°F) during your event, but 21 degrees Celsius (70°F), for example? We all know someone who, even after a good preparation, didn't reach their desired finish time due to the heat. Their training went well, their nutrition was tested, their recovery was fine, there were plenty of drinking stations on the way, but the weather threw a wrench into the works. Because, if you train at different temperatures than your event, you will have some issues during the race. You run the planned pace for the first half of your half or full marathon, and it feels fine. But once you've passed halfway, it turns out that you've started too fast, because the higher temperature makes it harder than expected.

Stryd has found a solution for that.

Once, I sat at the kitchen table with three running friends and showed them how Stryd's race calculator adjusts your race power to temperature, altitude, and humidity. They were flabbergasted. A week later everyone had bought a Stryd.

Below you'll see an example.

I let my Stryd know that I want to run a half marathon. Based on my Critical Power, Stryd calculates my race target power and my expected finish time:

So, I can run a half marathon with 265 Watts and my expected finish time will be 1:22:23. Stryd says that it can turn out 2 minutes faster or slower. For people who already run by power, the fact that I can run so fast with "only" 265 Watts is because I weigh "only" 59 kg (130 lbs).

Please note: it's of course not about the distance or the time, those are interchangeable.

Now for the interesting part.

Because, if I indicate that during my half marathon it's 21 degrees Celsius (70°F), and not 8 degrees Celsius (46°F), I get a different value. I should not run at 265 Watts, but at 259 Watts. Of course, my expected finish time becomes a bit slower. Instead of 1:22:23, the predicted time is now 1:24:32.

Figure 8

Figure 9

Figure 10

Additionally, if it's only 21 degrees Celsius (70°F) instead of the ideal 8 degrees Celsius (46°F), and if there are also some hills and an elevation of 230 meters, I have to adjust my power a little more. I won't run 259 Watts, but 257 Watts on my half marathon.

The race course altitude profile also ensures that my expected end time drops from 1:24:32 to 1:25:20.
This knowledge could have prevented many breakdowns for many people at events. If you know in advance, based on your training: the distance, the surface, the temperature, the height difference, and the humidity, then you'll know what performance you can reasonably expect on race day. And that is, of course, extremely valuable (and fun).

Summary Part II

To improve your personal best, if you have extra weight to lose and you do so healthily, 1% healthy weight loss makes your times 1% faster. Note: If you suffer from eating disorders, or other health complications, it's not a good idea to emphasize weight loss. Always consult with your doctor first.
Variation is the keyword in your training sessions: train in different zones.
Exercising slowly makes you faster.
Your fat stores are your largest energy source: learn to use it optimally.
Training intervals by power works better than training intervals by heart rate.
To predict what's possible for your 5K, 10K, half and full marathon, Stryd helps by analyzing the temperature and altitude difference for the specific course on race day.

Refreshment post at the BMW BERLIN-MARATHON (credits TUI Sports)

On your way to your PB

Y ou can translate any training plan from pace or heart rate
   to power.

What's not a good idea, however, is to combine training plans without consultation. Each plan has a balance between intensive training and easy training.
Periods of long runs and periods of fast workouts. Without a long term view
and without knowing the philosophy behind a plan, it's not wise to combine
two training plans on your own.

In the last part of this book we give tips per goal distance for how to train in
a targeted manner. If you've picked a training plan from the Internet, or if you
have training plans from a coach, it's always good to consult with your coach,
when in doubt. Normally, you can fit the tips in this chapter into your own
training plan. Of course, you can also use Stryd's own training plans.
There are many different schemes and streams in training theory. To check
whether a training plan works well for you, it's good to set a concrete goal and
check whether you're making progress. We recommend accelerating once a
month at a distance of 3 to 5 kilometers, if your body allows it. Does your
Critical Power increase? Then you're doing well. Or, if you find that your workouts feel better on your half or full marathon wattage, that's a good sign, too.
If you're a relatively novice runner (you've been running for less than 3 years),
you'll notice that progression affects all your distances. Are you training for a
half marathon? Then it may well be that you also improve your times on the 5K
and 10K. But if you've been running for a bit longer, then targeted training for
one distance is important. Because your basic speed is probably already so high
that specific training is needed.

Your paces for a half or full marathon are very different from your paces for a
5K or 10K distance.

In your training plan, a good mix of workouts on your race pace, alternated
with intervals and gentle workouts, is a good starting point.

The training plans in Stryd's app have been developed based on plans from
professional, respectable coaches. You'll immediately notice that the plans are

not expressed in kilometers, but in time. The reason for this is simple: the duration of your training is decisive for your muscles, tendons, ligaments, and joints. If a training plan is expressed in kilometers, then a workout of, for example, 10 kilometers is only 45 minutes for a fast runner, but for a novice runner with less aptitude, a workout of 10 kilometers requires more than one hour. To get someone with less experience to run longer than someone with a lot of experience - that would be strange. This "problem" can easily be solved by not giving runners a distance to train, but a duration. This way, 45 minutes is 45 minutes for everyone.

It's good to regularly train at your race pace during your training sessions, so you can get a feel for this pace for your race day.

How do you determine your race pace?

One of the things that makes Stryd so special, is the race power we wrote about earlier. In the app, you can enter the distance, and even the course you want to run, under the tab upcoming events. Once you've entered this, you immediately see the level of power at which you can run during the race. This is priceless. Headwind, uphill, temperature changes - with Stryd it doesn't matter. Your plan remains intact, because you know exactly what power level you can run at and that's always correct. An additional advantage is that you can train at race pace during your training. So whether you train for a PB at 5K, 10K, a half marathon or a full marathon, you know exactly what your competitive ability is and you can train these powers in your workouts, get used to them, and experience progression. Your race power will automatically increase as your Critical Power increases. You don't have to do anything special for that. No complicated formulas or calculations, Stryd calculates it for you and you can start training again. It's very exciting to see so clearly that your training is paying off.

How do you adjust your weight?

We already wrote about the impact of weight (mass) on your running performance. Two or three kilos less can make a big difference. With Critical Power, you can always see the power per kilogram of body weight/mass. For that number to be reliable and accurate, it's important to keep your weight up-to-date, because your expected finish time for your event will also change.

So, if you've lost some weight, you should adjust that in the settings (it's very nice to see your power per kilogram of body weight increase, without having to train so hard).

Note: you can adjust your weight in the app, near the battery. Click on the settings at the top right and a menu will open. You'll see Stryd with a battery icon next to it. Click on that, and when your app connects to your Stryd, you will see a header Update Height and Weight. Intuitively, this is not a logical place to enter your weight. You'd expect this to be under something like Profile, but it's not. The reason Stryd put weight under battery life is to make sure Stryd's app connects to your personal Stryd and not a roommate's or running friend's meter. Stryd must know what weight you have, otherwise it won't know how many kilos are moved at the measured speed (and temperature, wind, and altitude). That's why you can never lend your Stryd to a running buddy. With some watches, for example Garmin, you can also link to the serial number of your Stryd. This prevents person-to-person confusions with other runners who are running with a Stryd.

Note; do not change your weight to often. Small changes have little impact but disturbs your feeling with the power values you are used to.

In the next chapter, we'll describe the experiences of runners who've improved their personal bests by training with power in a targeted manner. You can't activate the training plans in Stryd itself, until you have your Critical Power.

Don't have Critical Power yet?

Go to Event in your Summary in the Stryd app. There, you can choose Intro to power instead of a distance. If you click on that, you'll get a workout that you can do to quickly and reliable determine a first approximation for your Critical Power.

3.1 Training for your 5K PB

The 5K is a beautiful distance.

Portrait: Anna P. (42) works for a major shoe brand and is the mother of two children. After her second baby, she didn't exercise much for three years. Little sleep, little time, no energy. Because Anna continued to eat chocolate and desserts, she never lost her pregnancy kilos. Three years after her second baby, she weighed 6 kilos (13 lbs) more than before her pregnancies. One day she decided: I want to lose some weight and I want to get fit again.

She got herself a good pair of running shoes and ran 2 or 3 times a week. Her motivation was great, and her discipline did the rest: she quickly lost three kilos (6.5 lbs) and built up her distances from 1 kilometer to 5 kilometers. She'll never forget the day she ran her first 5K race. Her children, her husband, and her mother were at the finish line, and the medal - in the shape of a gold 5 - hangs in the hall among the photos of her family. The local newspaper posted the results and times of all runners. She was proud that at 31:37 she left four more participants behind her. Her new goal: to run 5 kilometers under half an hour. Then, running became a struggle. She used to get better almost weekly and noticed that the improvement was easy to achieve. But now, she's been stuck on the same level. Her weight remained the same, and so did her pace. A friend recommended trying Stryd.

"Are you crazy, that's for you, because you run marathons. That's nothing for a snail like me," she said.

"The device just looks at your current level and then gives you tips to get better. It doesn't matter whether you train for a 5K within half an hour or whether you want to qualify for the Olympics."

Her frustration that she was no longer improving outweighed her hesitation to run with a power meter, so she tried it. Her power meter quickly taught her two things: she never ran slower than her favorite pace, and she never ran faster than her comfortable speed. Because of Stryd, she started combining easy workouts (which she did in the dark because she was embarrassed of her snail pace) with more intensive intervals. She had to run wattages she didn't think she could, but encouraged by Stryd's personal training plan, she gave it a try anyway. And it worked. She still ran 2 or 3 times a week, but due to the variation in pace, she was now improving rapidly. She ran her second 5 kilometer race in 27:38: an improvement of 4 minutes!

Want to try for yourself?

With Stryd you can go to Events in the main menu. There, you can enter 5 kilometers. Next, enter the date of your event and how many training sessions you want to do per week. Stryd also asks which day you have the most time, on that day you will get your longest workout in the plan.

Choose high volume or low volume, and your workouts are automatically added to your training calendar.

Two workouts are always a lot fun to do:

1. **Do a monthly "Critical Power boost training."**
    That is, a 3,000-meter workout session. This way, you'll test whether your critical power has increased.

2. **Run a block of at least 12 minutes every week on the wattage of your 5 kilometers.**
    This way, you get used to this power and you can check whether it feels good.

3.2 Training for your 10K PB

10 kilometers is the distance most often run. Setting a PB for 10K is a delicate task. It's a complex balance between starting fast enough and conserving your energy. Many runners tend to start a 10K too slowly, it's safe to say that if you can still accelerate after 6 kilometers, you've gone out too easy.

Running by power offers a solution. With your power meter, you won't start too fast or too slow.

Using Stryd for the first time, Koen set a new 10 kilometer PB. That's when he realized: Running by power is fascinating, more people should know about this!

Koen: My heart rate threshold is 192. Normally, I based my training on heart rate, and in races, I ran at the heart rate that matched that distance. I can run 10 kilometers at my heart rate threshold, so normally, I would start strong, go to my threshold and check occasionally to be sure it was below 192. This time, however, I didn't run by heart rate, but by power. My Critical Power is 270 Watts. So, I have to run the whole 10K at or slightly above 270 Watts. At 7 kilometers, Stryd began to make the difference for a new PB. Running at my Critical Power, I started to struggle and checked my watch. On my watch (which was paired with Stryd), I saw my power: 262 Watts. And I thought: I have to stay above 270 Watts. It was tough to do, but it worked. At that moment, if I had not run with power, and had only seen my heart rate, I certainly would not have been motivated to go a little faster. My heart rate was 193 at a pace of 3:58 min/km (5:45 min/mi). Normally, I would never accelerate. I would have thought: ouch, I'm going too fast. But Stryd knew exactly how fast I could really go. That surprised me. The first kilometers also offered Stryd an advantage over my heart rate. After 2 kilometers, I checked my watch, and I was running at 295 Watts: 25 Watts above Critical Power. I knew that this was a bit too enthusiastic. In the overview on Strava, however, I could see that my heart rate was still at 178, which was 14 beats below my threshold. So, the advantage of running by power is very valuable on race days: heart rate responds a bit slower, and it matters. The day after my PB, I spoke with an enthusiastic running coach.

"Aren't you over 40?" he asks a bit suspiciously.

"Yes, I'm turning 41 this month, why?" I ask.

"How can you still run PBs?" He sounds a little jealous.

But yes, that's the advantage for many runners who start running later in life. I've only been running seriously for five years, and with the accumulated running history and the knowledge of my body, I can improve for years to come.

Want to try for yourself?

In the Stryd app, you can go to Events in the main menu. In the PowerCenter on Stryd's website, you will find Events under Tools. There, you can enter 10 kilometers. Next, enter the date of your event and how many workouts you want to do per week. Stryd also asks which day you would like to do your longest run in the scheduled plan.

Choose high volume or low volume, and your workouts are automatically added to your training calendar.

These two workouts are always a lot of fun to do:

1. **Monthly Critical Power Maintenance Workout**

    This workout targets a 3 to 5 kilometer all out effort to help calibrate your Stryd Auto-Calculated Critical Power. This way, you can test if your Critical Power is improving.

2. **Interval Training Workout**

    This workout starts with a 15 minute warm up, then is 5 x 4:00 starting below your Stryd Auto-Calculated Critical Power and progressing to or slightly above your Stryd Auto-Calculated Critical Power (95%-102% of your CP). Your recovery in between each repeat is 2:00 at an easy effort (50-70% of your CP). After your last repeat, run an easy cool down.

3.3 Training for your half marathon PB

A half marathon is a popular distance among avid runners. It's the distance where you can really push your limits, and you still feel good for days after your intensive performance.

Jane S. (48) has been running since she was 12. From her 12th to her 41st birthday, she ran continuously. If she didn't run for a week, she would get sick. At that point, her husband would suggest that she might go for a quick run. However, at the age of 41, her world fell apart. She had been diagnosed with breast cancer. She overcame the disease with heavy operations, a lot of chemotherapy, and a good dose of willpower. At the age of 44, she set a goal: a half marathon. In her mind, finishing a half marathon was a definitive statement of health. She started training, but it was hard. She was used to fatigue, but not the kind of fatigue she felt after interval training. And she often had odd aches and pains. The fatigue and aches sparked fear and had her question herself. Am I still sick? Am I sick again?

After each check-up, her doctors assured her that she was healthy and that her condition was superb, given her circumstances.

She did an exercise test and started training with a heart rate monitor. That helped. Her pace went steadily from 5:30 min/km (8:30 min/mi) to under 5:00 min/km (8:00 min/mi). It wasn't quite the level she had hoped to achieve, but there was still progression. Then, she injured her knee and had to rest for a month. Jane had hoped to complete her half marathon after six months, but she'd been training for more than six months now, and she felt she hadn't made much progress. Then, one day her old coach asked to go for a run on the track with her. After a month of rest, her coach noticed that Jane was running at a lower step frequency than before. She ran 400 meters with a step frequency of 165 steps per minute. According to her coach, this should be at least 180 steps per minute. It felt awkward for Jane, and the coach suggested testing it with a Stryd meter. At which step frequency does she run the most economically? That was the question. It soon became clear that Jane benefited from a higher step frequency, and she started to learn more about her Critical Power. As it turned out, Jane had lost her natural technique after surgery and a long break. Tension from her neck and back radiated downward, and her left groin and left calf were also under high tension. Unconsciously, her body tried to correct that, and one of its "solutions" was a lower step frequency. Her new (mediocre) technique, however, combined with her old pace caused a serious injury. After rest and treatment of her back and groin, she could train freely again. She trained in a variety of ways and didn't pick up her pace until her Critical Power had increased. 14 months after her resolve to run a half marathon, she went for it. With a time of 1:42:46 she declared herself fit and healthy.

Want to try for yourself?

With Stryd you can go to Events in the main menu of the app. There, you can enter a half marathon. Next, enter the date of your event and the number of workouts you want to do each week. Stryd also asks which day you would like to perform your longest run in the training plan.

Choose high volume or low volume and your workouts are automatically added to your training calendar.

Examples of power-based workouts that make training enjoyable:

1. **Monthly Critical Power Maintenance Workout**
   This workout targets a 3 to 5 kilometer all out effort to help calibrate your Stryd Auto-Calculated Critical Power. This way, you can test if your Critical Power is improving.

2. **Workout with increasing power**
   This workout is an easy warm up with two sections of quality run-

ning. Your first quality section will be 20:00 at 88-95% of your Stryd Auto-Calculated Critical Power. You should aim to start the 20:00 between 88-90% and progress up to 95% by the end of the duration. After an easy 3:00 recovery you'll have a 10:00 section at the same power target, 88-95% of your Stryd Auto-Calculated Critical Power. The aim of this workout is to practice running at a steady submaximal effort for an extended duration. After the 10:00 section, run an easy cool down.

3.4 Training for your marathon PB

Covering 26.2 miles is the holy grail for many runners. A common question that marathon runners are asked is, what is your best time? And moments after crossing the line of your first marathon, you find yourself signing up for another one with the goal of running even faster. This was where 52 year-old Rick S. found himself.

After an injury at the age of 35, Rick retired from soccer and picked up running. He expanded his training and became more and more enthusiastic about what he was capable of. As a soccer player, he didn't like long distance running, but slowly, he became a fanatic. On Strava, he tracked all of his workouts and joined a running group. He started gaining mileage and getting faster. His trainer suggested running a marathon the year he turned 50. The age where the decline tends to become noticeable motivated Rick to prove otherwise. I'm still young and in the prime of my life. With a heart rate monitor and a focused plan, he ran the marathon in 4:08. Soon, Rick began to crunch the numbers. A marathon on flat terrain in October would give the opportunity to run under four hours. Moreover, Rick was able to lose 3 kilos, so a new project was born: a sub 4 marathon. Ignited by an enthusiastic user of Stryd in his running group, Rick also started running by power. He trained and lost weight and he set his eyes on his new running goal.

Rick decided to go for his second marathon in Amsterdam. The day before the marathon, he headed to the expo to pick up his racing bib. While there, he saw Ron and Stryd's Robijn at the Stryd exhibit. Rick talked passionately about his first marathon and the preparation he was taking for his second. His plan was to start out at 5:40 min/km (9:07 min/mi), which would lead him to running just under four hours. He was confident that his training set him up for the race day he had been dreaming of. Robijn asked why Rick wasn't planning to race by power. He was already training with power, so why not incorporate it into his race day plan? That was when Robijn showed Rick Stryd's Race Power Calculator. This tool calculated his ideal power target to aim for over the course of his marathon. Rick decided to give it a go and stuck with it throughout the race.

After the marathon, Rick had exciting news to share. Not only did he break the four hours barrier, but Rick ended up running 3:48! That is twelve minutes faster than his goal heading into the race.

This is a common success story of runners racing by power. Runners often vision their dream finishing time and train just enough to reach them. But, what if the goals that runners set for themselves are just at the cusp of their true capabilities? Running by power helps you reach your peak fitness and then go beyond what you thought you were capable of. At the age of 52, Rick is setting new personal bests in his half and full marathons and his PB journey has just begun!

What if you wake up on race morning and the wind is howling? You will need to adapt your race plan. But how do you adapt your plan at a moment's notice? The answer is Stryd. Stryd reports the extra power required to overcome air resistance. You will know how much power you need to run into a headwind, the power saved when running with a tailwind, and the power saved when drafting off a pack of runners. Stryd gives runners the ability to turn the wind into a measurable and performance enhancing force. All you have to do is stick to your power target. If you ignore power and solely focus on pace, you'll end up hitting the wall, and from that moment on, you'll lose a minute per kilometer.

Ready to get started?

When you are ready, head to the Stryd Mobile app and pick your target race distance, the date of your race, and enter how much time you have per week to commit to your training. Stryd will also ask which day works best for you to get your longest run in for the week. Continue to the next screen and you will be presented training plans personalized to fit your training and racing needs.

Choose one of the high volume or low volume plans and your workouts will automatically be added to your Stryd calendar.

Examples of power-based workouts that make training enjoyable:

1. **Monthly Critical Power Maintenance Workout**
   20 Minutes comfortably hard + 30 seconds very hard
   This workout targets a 20 minute pace and a 30 seconds all out effort to help calibrate your Stryd Auto-Calculated Critical Power and keep your power training zones up to date.

2. **Endurance-boosting Workouts**
   3 Miles 85% of CP, 2 miles at 90% of CP, 1 mile at 95% of CP
   This progression workout is designed to build your aerobic capacity to power through to the end of your next race.

Are you currently following your own training plan, but interested in running by power? Any training plan can easily be converted into a plan backed by running power. Hans and Ron explain how. Let's say, for example, your training plan schedules a 10 kilometer run at your race pace. You weigh 70 kg and run 10 km in 50:00. Your training prescribes you to run at a pace of 5:00 min/km (8:02 min/mi). Over 1000 meters (1 km), that is 300 seconds (5:00), so 1000/300 = 3.33 meters/second. The wattage (power) with which you have to run is 3.33 m/s * 1.04 * 70 kg = 242 Watts.
Another example workout could be that your plan schedules you to run 400 meters in 28 seconds per 100 meters.
You then run 100/28 = 3.57 m/s. Your corresponding wattage is 3.57 m/s * 1.04 * 70 kg = 260 Watts.
As you can see, any training session can be easily converted into a plan based on running power. Whether you have an endurance run, blocks, or intervals over a certain distance or duration, you can calculate the wattage you need to aim for in all training scenarios.
You can import each of these training sessions directly on your watch for real-time guidance.

DO YOU TRAIN BY THE STANS VAN DER POEL 14 KILOMETER PLAN?

You can convert Stans van der Poel's famous 14 kilometer training schedule into a plan based on running power within seconds.

A few years back, one of us (KdJ) wrote a book together with Stans van der Poel - The Running Revolution - in which you train no more than 10 kilometers for a half marathon and no more than 14 kilometers for a full marathon. At first, the training plan was received with skepticism, and experienced runners thought it was ridiculous. But after testing by a Runner's World magazine journalist and a journalist of the daily newspaper De Volkskrant, the prevailing feeling about the plan shifted. Running a marathon with a maximum training distance of only 14 kilometers is possible. Originally, runners believed that running a marathon off of this type of training was possible but that a fast finishing time was out of reach. This all changed when Koen ran the Amsterdam marathon a bit faster than three hours while training by Stans van der Poel's plan. Now, the 14 kilometer training plan of Stans van der Poel has become a household name in the Netherlands. Runners who followed the plan found that while you train fewer kilometers, it's not an easy schedule or a quick fix for bucket list runners. Because, the big secret of the scheme is marathon heart rate. You train fewer kilometers, but you train more in your marathon heart rate zone. Stans van der Poel explains how you can determine your goal marathon heart rate and plans your training accordingly. Half of your training is done at race pace. The plan is therefore milder for slow runners than for fast runners.

While Stryd's training is quite different from Stans van der Poel's training approach, you can still incorporate running power into these plans. Running power compliments Stans van der Poel plans perfectly to help you reach peak fitness on race day. Instead of doing your training at your marathon heart rate, you can easily do the training by your marathon power. You can find your target marathon power by heading to the Stryd Mobile app and adding an upcoming event. Stryd will calculate your marathon target power which you can then supplement into your current training plan.

FROM THEORY TO PRACTICE

Back-
grounds

4.1 Energy

In this book the laws of physics and physiology are used to study running, so we can understand the fundamental factors that determine our performance. In running we use a certain amount of energy (E), which of course depends on the distance.

Our muscles and our heart-lung system provide this energy: we will call this our 'human engine'. Our human engine has a certain capacity or power (P), which is the amount of energy per unit of time. Elite athletes obviously have a human engine with more power than ordinary people, so they can run faster. The general relationship is that you can calculate your race time (t) for a certain distance if you know the power (P) of your human engine and how much net energy (E) is required to run that distance:

t = E/P

Example for the Marathon:
E = 2961 kiloJoules (net), P = 235 Watts, t = 2,961,000/235 = 12,600 seconds = 3 hours 30 minutes.

Of course, the trick is to know the numerical values of E and P. Once you know these, you can calculate your race time easily. In later chapters we will elucidate on which factors these values depend. With this knowledge, you will be able to understand which factors determine your racing performance. So you can also make a more informed decision on what you can do to improve your performance.

We will also prove that the numbers in the example are exactly right for our Marathon Man; a hypothetical man - sorry ladies - of 35 years who runs the marathon in 3 hours and 30 minutes and weighs 70 kg. We use the Marathon Man frequently to illustrate the impact of various factors on his race times. In this chapter, we will first discuss the concept of energy (E). We will give some examples from daily life and illustrate how you can use the concept of energy to make useful calculations.

Energy in our food

The concept of energy is best known in daily life from the amount of kilo-calories (kcal) in our food. Most readers will be aware that we consume some 2500 kcal daily (of course heavyweight champion Tyson Fury will consume much more than supermodel Naomi Campbell). As 1 kcal is equivalent to 4,184 kilo Joule (kJ), we can calculate that 2500 kcal equals 10,460 kJ.

Weight loss resulting from the marathon

We should note that the efficiency of our human engine (the metabolic efficiency) is around 25%. This means that the gross energy consumption of our body is 4 times the net energy use of running. Consequently, our Marathon Man uses a total of 4*2961 = 11,844 kJ of metabolic energy to run the marathon.

When we compare this to his daily food consumption of 10,460 kJ, we can calculate that the energy requirement of the marathon is only 11,884/10,460 = 113% of the daily energy (calorie) intake with his food. Obviously, running a marathon will not result in a large weight loss (apart from the weight loss from sweating; this will be quickly replenished by drinking water or sports drinks).

How much weight do you actually lose from running a marathon? We can calculate this when we realize that our body fat has an energy density of 9 kcal/gram or 37.6 kJ/gram. Consequently, the Marathon Man will lose 11,844/37.6 = 316 grams of body fat. A modest amount which may not inspire heavyweights to run a marathon as a means to lose body fat! Of course, in the long run daily training will definitely lead to a sizable and stable weight loss, as many runners have experienced.

Energy in our daily life

At home, the concept of energy is best known to many of us from the electricity consumption (in kWh) for lighting, the fridge and other household uses. When we realize that 1 kWh is equivalent to 3600 kJ, we can calculate that the amount of energy in our daily food is equivalent to 10,460/3600 = 2.9 kWh. A very small number indeed, in particular when we consider that 1 kWh costs only some 0.135 US$. In theory, we would thus need only 2.9*0.135 = 0.39 US$ to provide the daily energy for our metabolism. It is a pity that we cannot eat electricity as this would be a lot cheaper than our groceries!

Another example from daily life is the gas consumption of our cars. The energy density of petrol is 28,800 kJ/l, so if we could drink petrol we would need only 10,460/28,800 = 0.4 liter per day! With a gas price of some 0.6 US$/l, our daily cost would be as low as 0.4*0.6 = 0.24 US$, so even cheaper than electricity! Of course the energy density of petrol is quite high, which we can see when we calculate that the energy content of a small car tank of 40 liter is equivalent to 40*28,800 = 1,152,000 kJ. This is the same amount of energy that we consume with our food in 1,152,000/10,460 = 110 days! Apparently, the gas mileage of our body is far superior to that of our car!

How much energy do we use for running?

When we neglect the air-resistance, we can calculate the energy cost of running with the formula:

E = cmd

The numerical value of the specific energy cost of running (c) can be set at 0.98 kJ/kg/km. The body weight (m) of our Marathon Man is 70 kg, so the energy cost of running a marathon (d = 42.195K) is 0.98*70*42.194 = 2985 kJ. The figure shows the energy cost of running as a function of the distance (for the Marathon Man, 70 kg and neglecting the air-resistance).

How long do you need to run in order to lose 1 kg of body fat? We can calculate that easily as 1 kg of body fat is equivalent to 37,600 kJ. Taking into account the metabolic efficiency of 25%, the Marathon Man needs to run d = E/cm = (37,600/(0,98*70*0.25) = 137 km to burn 1 kg of body fat!

So for such a small effect you seem to have to invest a lot of effort, but with regular training you will reach this easily, so you will definitely lose weight (provided you do not increase your food consumption of course).

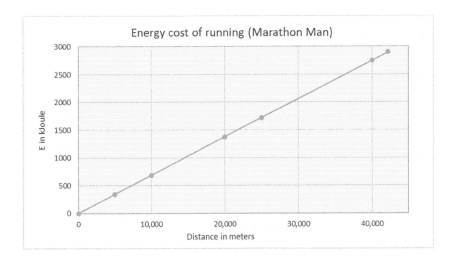

4.2 Power

In the previous chapter, we gave the formula in its simplest form to calculate your race time (t) for any distance, once you know the power (P) of your human engine and the energy cost (E) of running that distance:

t = E/P

Example for the marathon:
E = 2961 kiloJoules, P = 235 Watts, t = 2,961,000/235 = 12,600 seconds = 3 hours 30 minutes.

In this chapter, we will look more closely at the concept of power (P). Once again, we will give some examples from daily life and illustrate how you can use the concept of power to make useful calculations.

The average power of the human engine

One way to approach this is by simply dividing the daily energy intake from our food (E = 10,460 kJ) by the number of seconds in a day (t = 86,400 sec). The result is an average power (P) of 121 Watts, about equivalent to an (old-fashioned) lightbulb.

However, we should realize that this is just a theoretical calculation of the average 'thermal' power. In practice, we need to take into account that the metabolic efficiency is only some 25%, so the average 'mechanical' power of the human engine is just 121*0.25 = 30 Watts.

Of course our human engine is quite capable of supplying more power during a short time. As an example we mention the fact that a professionals cyclist pushed 415 Watts during 39 minutes while climbing to the summit of the Alpe d'Huez in the Tour de France.

We can appreciate the meaning of 30 Watts by considering that we use it to produce electricity with a home trainer. If we would cycle an entire working day (8 hours), we would produce 8*30/1000 = 0.24 kWh of electricity, with a monetary value of just 0.24*0.135 = 0.03 US$!

Other examples of power

In 1777, James Watts defined the unit of horse power (HP) as the amount of power that a horse produces by hoisting a weight of 150 kg up a height of 30 meters in 1 minute. The energy cost of this can be calculates as:

E = mgh

With the gravity constant g = 9.81 m/s² , E becomes 150*9.81*30 = 44,145 Joule.

Consequently, the HP is equivalent to:

P = E/t = 44,145/60 = 736 Watts

As we know that a horse can easily maintain this power, we may conclude that the power of the horse engine is substantially larger than that of the human engine. The power of modern cars is much higher still. Many a car is equipped with an engine of 200 HP or 147,200 Watts. In the previous chapter, we saw already that the energy content of a small 40 liter car tank of petrol is equivalent to 40*28,800 = 1,152,000 kJ. Consequently, we can conclude that the tank will be empty after a time t = E/P = 1,152,000/147,200/3600 = 2,1 hour drive at full power.

How can you calculate your race time in running?

In the previous chapter we already saw the formula to calculate the energy cost of running a flat course:

E = cmd

This means that for our Marathon Man the energy cost of running 1K is equal to 0.98*70*1 = 68.7 kJ (c = 0.98 kJ/kg/km, m = 70 kg). When we know his power P, we can calculate his race time with the formula:

t = E/P

In this chapter we will simply assume that Marathon Man's power is constant and equal to 235 Watts. With this assumption, we can calculate that his time per km will be 68,700/235 = 292 seconds or 4 minutes 52 seconds. The figure below gives the race time as a function of the distance.

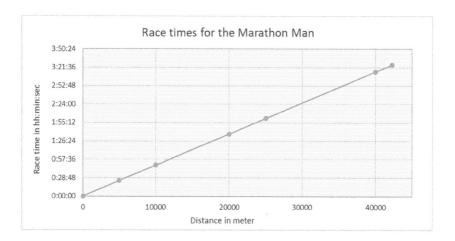

We should note that the figure is the result of some simplifications:
1. We have not yet taken into account the effect of the air-resistance. This has a small, but not negligible impact.
2. In practice the power will not be constant, but decline with time. As a result of this, the race times at short distances will be better than calculated.

In later chapters, both aspects will be taken into account, so exact running times can be calculated.

4.3 The running model

So far we have used very simple models to calculate the race times based on the available power P (in Watts) of the human engine. This has already given promising and interesting results. Now we introduce you the complete model of the physics of running. In order to do this, we need to know how much power is needed to run in different conditions.

Obviously, additional power is required to run against the wind. Consequently, we need to know the amount of power required to overcome the air-resistance P_a (in Watts). Running against a hill also requires additional power, so we need to know the amount of power required to overcome the climbing resistance P_c (in Watts). Running on a flat course without any air-resistance of course also requires power. By analogy we call this the amount of power required to overcome the running resistance P_r (in Watts). The figure below illustrates our running model.

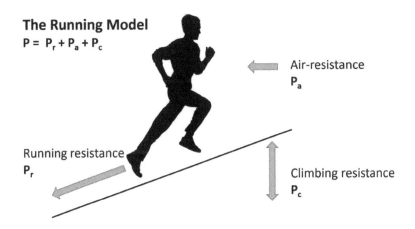

The Running Model
$P = P_r + P_a + P_c$

Air-resistance
P_a

Running resistance
P_r

Climbing resistance
P_c

In the equilibrium situation, the available power of the human engine should be equal to the sum of the power required to overcome these 3 resistances: the running resistance, the air-resistance and the climbing resistance:

$$P = P_r + P_a + P_c$$

We call this the running model. In this chapter we will analyze the 3 resistances that define the running model.

The Running Resistance

Theoretically, we can calculate the amount of power P_r (in Watts) required to overcome the running resistance from the specific energy cost of running c (in kJ/kg/km), the body weight m (in kg) and the speed v (in m/s) of the runner, as given in the box.

> ### The Running Resistance
>
> $$P_r = cmv$$
>
> Example:
> c = 0.98 kJ/kg/km, m = 70 kg , v = 12.06 km/h
> P_r = 0.98*70*12.06/3.6 = 230 watts

The example is valid for our Marathon Man, who weighs 70 kg and runs the marathon in 3 hours and 30 minutes, so with a speed of 12.06 km/h. A sound value for c is 0.98 kJ/kg/km (for the average runner).

We can also relate the specific energy cost c to the notion of the running economy (RE), which is used to describe the amount of energy used in running. The RE is usually given as the specific amount of oxygen used (in ml O_2/kg/km).

As 1 ml O_2 has an energy value of 19.5 Joule, so with the muscle efficiency of 25%, we can calculate that a c-value of 0.98 kJ/kg/km is equivalent to an RE of 0.98*1000/19.5/0.25 = 201 ml O_2/kg/km. In later chapters we will discuss how you can improve your RE and reduce your c-value, so you will need less energy and run more economically.

The formula for the running resistance shows that the required power is directly proportional to the body weight and the speed, see the figure below.

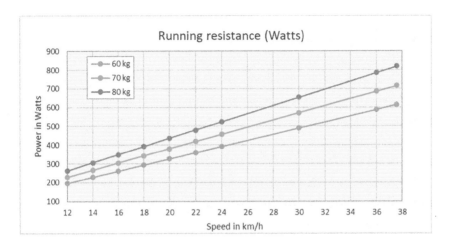

The figure shows that for sprinters the required power is quite high. When we look at the numbers of Usain Bolt (world record 100 meter in 9.58 seconds, so a speed of 37.6 km/h and a body weight of 94 kg), we can calculate that his running resistance has been 963 Watts. And this number does not even include the air-resistance and the power required for his initial acceleration!

As the formula shows, the specific power (in Watts/kg) determines the achievable speed, as shown in the figure below.

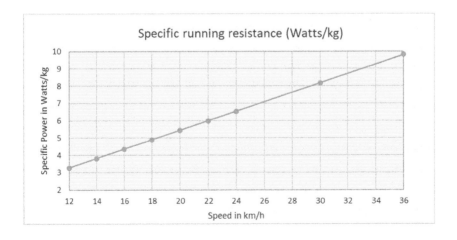

The figure shows that in order to achieve a speed of 20 km/h, a runner should be able to mobilize at least a specific power of 5.45 Watts/kg. Also this number does not yet include the air-resistance!

The Air-Resistance

The power P_a (in Watts) required to overcome the air-resistance depends on the air density ρ (in kg/m³), the air-resistance factor c_dA (in m²), the speed v (in m/s) and the wind speed v_w (in m/s), as shown in the box.

> ### The Air Resistance
>
> $P_a = 0.5\rho c_d A(v+v_w)^2 v$
>
> Example:
> $\rho = 1.205$ kg/m³, $c_dA = 0.24$m², v = 12.06 km/h, $v_w = 0$ km/h
> $P_a = 0.5*1.205*0.24*(12.06/3,6)^3 = 5$ watts

The example is valid again for our Marathon Man, who runs at a temperature of 20°C (at this temperature the density of the air is 1.205 kg/m³) and in ideal, windless conditions. We see that the power P_a (in Watts) required to overcome the air-resistance due to his 'own' wind is rather small, 5 Watts or 2% of his run-

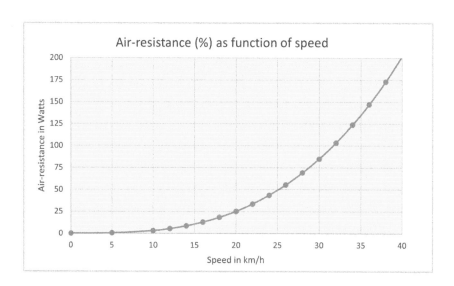

ning resistance P_r of 230 Watts. However, the formula also shows that P_a increases to the 3rd power of the speed. Consequently, the impact of the air-resistance is much higher for elite runners, as can be seen in the figure above.

The figure shows that for sprinters P_a is quite high. When we look at the numbers of Usain Bolt (100 meter in 9.58 seconds, so a speed of 37.6 km/h and a body weight of 94 kg), we can calculate that his P_a has been 167 Watts or 17% of his P_r of 963 Watts. This also means that Usain could easily improve his world record if he would run at altitude. In other chapters we will show the impact on the race times of the other factors that impact P_a, such as the wind conditions and the help of pace makers.

The Climbing Resistance

The climbing resistance depends on the gradient i (in %), the body weight m (in kg) and the speed v (in m/s), as shown in the box.

The Climbing Resistance

$P_c = (i/100)mgv$

Example:
$i = 7.4\%$, $m = 70$ kg, $v = 12.06$ km/h, $g = 9.81$ m/s^2
$P_c = 7.4/100*70*9.81*12.06/3.6 = 170$ watts

The example is valid again for the Marathon Man, who attempts to run to the top of the Alpe d'Huez in France. The numbers show that uphill he cannot maintain a speed of 12.06 km/h, as this would require a climbing resistance of 170 Watts on top of the 230 Watts that he needs for the running resistance and the 5 Watts for the air-resistance.

So he will have to reduce his speed until the sum of the 3 resistances equals the power of his human engine (235 Watts for the Marathon Man). In reality the muscle efficiency is slightly higher uphill than at a flat course, so P_c is somewhat less than follows from the theoretical formula.

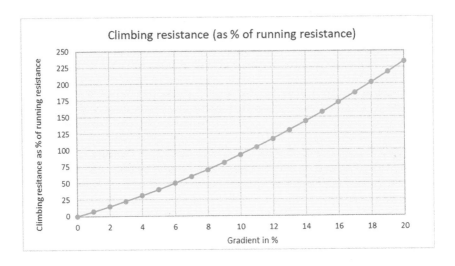

The climbing resistance P_c (in Watts) increases proportionally with the speed v and the gradient i, as can be seen from the formula. As the running resistance P_r (in Watts) also increases proportionally with the speed v, the ratio of P_c/P_r depends only on the gradient i. This ratio is given in the figure below. There are more factors that impact the climbing resistance and the speed uphill and downhill. We have included it in the model calculations in this book and in our computer program.

Conclusions

The physics of running comprises the formulas that describe the 3 resistances. In the equilibrium situation, the power output of the human engine will be equal to the sum of these 3 resistances: the running resistance, the air-resistance and the climbing resistance:

$$P = P_r + P_a + P_c$$

The final result is the fairly complicated 3rd power formula given in the box below. In the next chapter we will explain how we have solved this equation. There we will also show how we can use the formula to calculate the attainable speed and race time depending on the power of the human engine and the race conditions.

The Physics of Running

Running resistance:	$P_r = cmv$
Air resistance:	$P_a = 0.5\rho c_d A(v+v_w)^2 v$
Climbing resistance:	$P_c = (i/100)mgv$
Running formula:	$P = cmv + 0.5\rho c_d A(v+v_w)^2 v + (i/100)mgv$

4.4 The FTP (CP60)

In middle and long distance running, the Functional Threshold Power (FTP) is one of the most important factors determining your performance. The FTP is defined as the power output that can be maintained for 1 hour and is expressed in Watts per kg of body weight.

So FTP is equivalent to CP60 as mentioned in the first parts of this book. CP60 is the critical power you can keep up for 60 minutes. Some use a slightly different definition for FTP, but you will understand after reading this book that this is the most useful definition for endurance sports.

The term functional threshold is used because above this level lactate (lactic acid) starts to accumulate in your muscles. This means that if you go beyond the FTP intensity level, your muscles will start to acidify and you will not be able to maintain your speed.

This also means that at the FTP level, your muscles will still produce power with the aerobic energy systems. In practice, the fuel mix at the FTP level will be about 75% glycogen and 25% fatty acids. Consequently, the share of glycogen will be less than at the VO_2 max level, where it is 90%. This also means that your power output and speed will be less than at the VO_2 max level. This makes sense as you can maintain the VO_2 max level for no more than 10 minutes. There is a fixed relationship between the FTP and the VO_2 max. We summarized this in the box below.

Relationship Between FTP and VO$_2$ max

FTP = 0.88*0.25*VO$_2$ max*19.55/60

FTP = 0.072*VO$_2$ max

Example: VO$_2$ max = 51 ml/kg/min

FTP = 0.072*51 = 3.67 watts/kg

How can the FTP be determined?

Traditionally the FTP is determined in cycling. Bikes can be equipped with power meters that enable the determination of the FTP, both in the field and in the lab. A practical problem is that it is not easy to go all out for 1 hour. This is not something you want to do regularly.

Fortunately, we can estimate the FTP from a shorter test as well. The FTP is equal to 93% of the power that can be maintained for 20 minutes or 88% of the power that can be maintained for 10 minutes. An all-out test of 10 or 20 minutes can be incorporated in most training programs.

When performed in the lab (e.g. a Sports Medical Advice Center), the FTP test can be combined with additional tests and measurements, like the oxygen uptake and the lactate production, which will give a more complete picture of your fitness and performance level.

How can the FTP be determined in running?

Until recently, it was not possible to measure the power while running. However, presently there are running power meters available on the market. These power meters do not measure forces as with power meters for cyclists. Running power meters as Stryd actually measure movements in 3 dimension by means of Inertial Measurement Units. IMUs contain sensors such as accelerometers, gyroscopes, and more. These data are used to calculate the power by means of advanced algorithms. This is based on the same theory as explained in this book. Garmin, Polar and Coros use GPS as one of the main parameters to calculate running power.

In the present chapter, we will discuss how you can calculate your FTP based on your race times at different distances, both in the field and on a treadmill. As we saw earlier, your specific running resistance in Watts/kg is directly proportional to your speed:

$$P_r/m = cv$$

This formula is valid in a situation without air-resistance, so on a treadmill. With c = 0.98 kJ/kg/km and v expressed in km/h, the formula becomes:

$$P_r/m = 0.27*v$$

This relationship is shown in the figure.

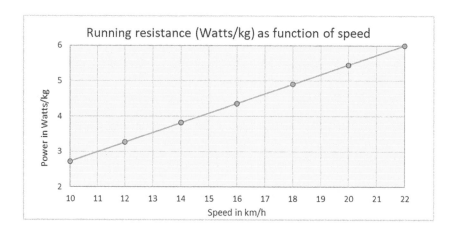

Now all you have to do is to correct for the duration of the test, as the FTP is equivalent to a 1 hour test. As an example, we use a test of 5 minutes only. The correction factor should then be $(5/60)^{-0.07} = 0.84$.

Let's say you run 15 km/h during these 5 minutes. According to the formula, your specific power at 15 km/h is 0.27*15 = 4.05 Watts/kg. Your FTP thus becomes 0.84*4.05 = 3.40 Watts/kg. We note that it is better to do the test during a somewhat longer period, 10 or 20 minutes, to limit the impact of the anaerobic energy systems of your human motor.

Which factors determine your FTP?

In literature and in practice, it has been established that the FTP depends on the same factors as the VO_2 max:

- Talent (if you want to be a great runner, you should choose your parents carefully).
- Sex (the FTP of men is 10-15% higher than the one of women).
- Age (the FTP decreases approximately 0.5-1.0 % per year over the age of 35).
- Training (the FTP can be increased by some 5-25% as a result of training).
- Weight (the FTP is inversely proportional to the body weight, so shedding excess body fat will increase your FTP).

The FTP of the world record holders is in the order of 6.4 Watts/kg, as we have shown in an earlier chapter. Athletes like Haile Gebrselassie and Mo Farrah reach these values as a result of a combination of talent and years of meticulous training. Normal values for young men are around 3.1 - 4.2, for young women these values are 2.6 - 3.6 Watts/kg.

Consequently, 'normal' persons can never reach the values of Haile and Mo, not even with the most fanatical training. The table below gives a classification of FTP levels that is used frequently.

Power Levels of Men and Women			
Classification		FTP Men (Watts/kg)	FTP Women (Watts/kg)
Absolute top	100%	6.4	5.7
International	90%	5.8	5.1
National	80%	5.1	4.6
Regional	70%	4.5	4.0
Running Enthusiast	60%	3.8	3.4
Fitness Runner	50%	3.2	2.9
Untrained	40%	2.6	2.3
Poor	30%	1.9	1.7
Very poor	20%	1.4	1.1

How can you use your FTP to predict your running times?

On the Internet many calculators can be found that predict cycling times at various distances as a function of the FTP. For running such calculators do not yet exist. However, in later chapters, we will show exactly what the relationship is between your FTP and your running times. We have also developed a calculator at www.theSecretofRunning.com which can be used to assess your FTP and predict your running times at different distances and in various conditions.

4.5 Improve your performance index? Lose some body weight!

Many runners like to know what their level is. Others just like to run in the great outdoors. They know who they always stay ahead of and who they can't keep up with.

To make a fair comparison, you must of course correct for the impact of age. If you train from an early age, you are fastest around 30 years of age. After that, your performance will gradually decrease over the years. After you reach the age of 70, you deteriorate even faster. And of course there is a difference between men and women. The physical performance of women is less than that of men; the most important reason is the smaller amount of muscles.

Level playing field

For the most fair comparison of your running level it is therefore necessary to take into account age and gender. But how do you do that? The solution is simple. You can express your running power in a number.

We take power literally: we use the wattage you can maintain for an hour. This wattage is called the functional threshold power (FTP) and is per kg body weight. Hans' FTP is 4.3 Watts/kg and Ron's is currently 3.7 Watts/kg. So the 67-year old Hans is a better runner than the 64 year old Ron. If the FTP of both would be the same, Hans would still be better because of the age difference.

How do you get to know your FTP?

Don't worry, you don't necessarily have to run as fast as you can for an hour with a running power meter. We have a calculator with which you can calculate your FTP with your data from a fast training or race.

In the calculator at www.theSecretofRunning.com you fill in the distance of your run - at least 3 km - and your time and weight. Under tab 'VO$_2$ max and FTP' you can read what your FTP is per kg body weight, in Watts/kg, and what your VO$_2$ max is as milliliters of oxygen per kg body weight per minute. Remember: Per kilogram of body weight!

Performance index by age and body weight

FTP is a measure of the power of your human engine, lungs, heart and oxygen transport system. If you lose weight, the power of your human engine does not change. Per kilogram of body weight it becomes higher!

An example. Ron's FTP is currently 3.7 Watts/kg. Ron weighs 80 kg. His human engine can deliver 3.7*80 = 296 Watts for one hour. When Ron trains for a marathon, he loses some weight to 78 kg. His FTP is then 296/78 = 3.8 Watts/kg. He is therefore 2.5% (2/80 is 2.5%) faster. Over a kilometer that makes him more than 10 seconds faster. On the marathon it is 7 minutes. That is worth the effort!

If Ron doesn't train a lot during the seasonal holidays and eats and drinks a lot, he might weigh as much as 84 kg at the beginning of January .....
His FTP will then be 296/84 = 3.5 Watt/kg. He will no longer be in the regional category for his age, but a recreational runner. And worse, on the marathon suddenly 5% (4/80 is 5%) slower. That comes down to 15 seconds per kilometer. Over the whole marathon that means a nearly 11 minutes! If you want to know the impact of your weight on your times, you can calculate it yourselves now.

Of course, this example is not a plea to lose weight without restrictions. Pay attention to your Body Mass Index (BMI) and body fat percentage. Keep it healthy!

Power Levels of Men							
Classification		FTP (Watts/kg) 30 years	FTP (Watts/kg) 40 years	FTP (Watts/kg) 50 years	FTP (Watts/kg) 60 years	FTP (Watts/kg) 70 years	FTP (Watts/kg) 80 years
World class	100%	6.4	6.0	5.6	5.2	4.7	4.0
International	90%	5.7	5.4	5.1	4.7	4.2	3.6
National	80%	5.1	4.8	4.5	4.2	3.8	3.2
Regional	70%	4.5	4.2	3.9	3.6	3.3	2.8
Recreational	60%	3.8	3.6	3.4	3.1	2.8	2.4
Fair	50%	3.2	3.0	2.8	2.6	2.4	2.0
Untrained	40%	2.5	2.4	2.2	2.1	1.9	1.6
Poor	30%	1.9	1.8	1.7	1.6	1.4	1.2
Dramatic	20%	1.3	1.2	1.1	1.0	0.9	0.8

Power Levels of Women							
Classification		FTP (Watts/kg) 30 years	FTP (Watts/kg) 40 years	FTP (Watts/kg) 50 years	FTP (Watts/kg) 60 years	FTP (Watts/kg) 70 years	FTP (Watts/kg) 80 years
World class	100%	5.7	5.4	5.0	4.6	4.2	3.6
International	90%	5.1	4.8	4.5	4.2	3.7	3.2
National	80%	4.6	4.3	4.0	3.7	3.3	2.9
Regional	70%	4.0	3.8	3.5	3.2	2.9	2.5
Recreational	60%	3.4	3.2	3.0	2.8	2.5	2.2
Fair	50%	2.9	2.7	2.5	2.3	2.1	1.8
Untrained	40%	2.3	2.1	2.0	1.8	1.7	1.4
Poor	30%	1.7	1.6	1.5	1.4	1.2	1.1
Dramatic	20%	1.1	1.1	1.0	0.9	0.8	0.7

4.6 The impact of the running surface on your pace

Many races are run on a fast track. That is, as everyone knows from experience, on asphalt roads or on a synthetic athletics track. In both cases, the surface is hard and flat. These are the best. The running resistance is minimal and the specific Energy Cost of Running (ECOR) in these conditions for a trained runner is 1.04 kJ/kg/km. This value includes the drag from your 'own' running wind.

Experienced runners know that it can already make a difference if uneven segments with stones or boulders are included in the course. This is especially true if you have to cross sections of forest land or even loose sand. What is the impact of the running surface on performance? How much time are you losing?

Constant power

Different from a cycling power meter with a running power meter a power meter for a bike calculates the power from the force you actually put on your pedals. Running power meters determine the running power with the tiny IMUs with accelerometers and a wind speedometer in the foot pod attached to your laces (Stryd) or with GPS and barometer (Garmin, Polar, COROS, iPhone apps and others). For this reason a running power meter does not see any differences in surface.

On a hard surface constant power works with elevation changes in the course. Your fastest time will be run if you constantly focus on your achievable power for that distance along the way. You then consciously run slower uphill, don't arrive at the top out of breath with a red face, and go downhill with a faster than average pace. The same is true with a headwind and a tailwind. For your fastest time you run with a constant power all the time.

Running in loose sand can require more than 25% extra energy. You won't be able to sustain that. You will therefore have to slow down your pace and maintain a lower power value on your running watch. Different from a cycling power meter with a running power meter how much lower you will have to estimate yourself.

Additional resistance of sand, grass and forest soil

There are several publications in the literature about the specific energy consumption for different surfaces. For example, the energy consumption of a forest course can be about 3% higher and of a cross course even in the order of 6% higher. These values correspond well with our experiences. With all running power meters the (in this case average) power to be maintained should be reduced by the same percentage.

Loss of time on a non-ideal course

In the table below, we show the results of calculations on the following cases:
• Ideal course (asphalt, synthetic)
• Forest course (mix of bike paths and grass, 3% higher)
• Cross (mix of grass and sand, 6% higher)

Of course these are schematized situations and the course will differ in practice from these assumptions, but it does give a good impression of the impacts. In the table the impact of the course on the times for our Marathon Man is calculated.

The Marathon Man is the example runner we use in our book The Secret of Running and in many of our articles. With his 70 kg body weight, he runs the marathon in 3:30 hours.

We see that the effect of the course for our Marathon Man can be about 1 to 2 minutes on the 10K and 2 to 10 minutes at the marathon. A marathon is not often run on a cross-track, so the differences in practice are less large.

Impact running surface Marathon Man			
Distance (km)	Ideal (hrs:min:sec)	Dirt trail (hrs:min:sec)	Cross country (hrs:min:sec)
0.8	0:03:04	0:03:09	0:03:14
1.5	0:05:59	0:06:09	0:06:19
3	0:12:32	0:12:52	0:13:13
5	0:21:36	0:22:11	0:22:47
10	0:45:13	0:46:28	0:47:44
15	1:09:41	1:11:37	1:13:33
20	1:34:42	1:37:20	1:39:59
21.1	1:40:16	1:43:04	1:45:52
25	2:00:09	2:03:30	2:06:52
30	2:25:57	2:30:01	2:34:07
42.195	3:30:00	3:35:53	3:41:48

4.7 How much time do you lose due to curves and turns?

In our columns at www.theSecretofRunning.com we discussed the spectacular developments in recent years in the quest of running the marathon sub 2 hours. As you will know, Eliud Kipchoge finally succeeded with his phenomenal 1:59:40 in Vienna at October 12, 2019. A fantastic performance that is rightly viewed by all marathon runners with the greatest awe.

In the search for the marathon sub 2 hours, sponsors and scientists have made every effort to maximize the chances. A very important success factor in Vienna was undoubtedly the reduction of the air resistance by the team of 41 pacers, who drafted Eliud in a sophisticated manner. They used an aerodynamically optimized reversed V-formation as described in the chapter The physiology of Eliud Kipchoge and his 'Breaking2' pacers.

In various columns we have explained the importance of the air-resistance on the performance in running. We have also discussed the impact of other factors, such as the running shoes (including the success shoes Nike Vaporfly), differences in elevation (including the idea of running a marathon completely downhill), wind (including the idea of running a marathon with a tail wind only) and the subsurface (it will not be easy to find a faster subsurface than asphalt in practice).

The organizers of the big city marathons try to design their course as optimally as possible within the limits set by the IAAF (for example, the finish should not be more than 42 meters lower than the start to limit the impact of the elevation gain and the finish should not be more than 21.1 km from the start to limit the impact of tailwind). Recognized fast marathons such as Berlin, Valencia, Rotterdam and Amsterdam have a course that is almost completely flat and asphalted. The organizers are constantly trying to make their course even faster by avoiding overpasses, cobblestones and other disturbing influences.

In this chapter we elaborate on a often mentioned factor, namely the loss of time due to curves and turns. Berlin is praised for the long straight roads, so that the impact of the curves would be minimal. But how big is the time loss due to curves and turns and what differences can it cause in practice?

Theory time losses due to curves and turns

As reader you will be aware of our running model, which we have described earlier in this book. Again the figure below shows the basic concept of the model, namely that the power of the human engine P must be equal to the sum of the powers required to surmount the running resistance P_r, the air resistance P_a and the climbing resistance P_c.

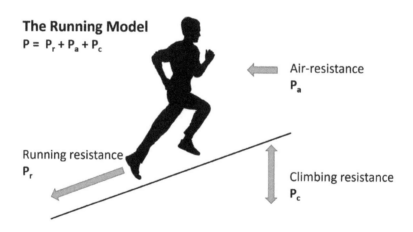

The Running Model
$$P = P_r + P_a + P_c$$

Air-resistance P_a

Running resistance P_r

Climbing resistance P_c

As you train more and better, the power of your human engine P will increase so you will have more power available to overcome the 3 resistances, allowing you to run faster. As everyone will understand, your running power P depends on the duration of the effort and therefore the distance: at a longer distance you have to slow down somewhat so apparently your running power is lower.

The full running model is summarized in the box below.

$$P = cmv + 0.5\rho c_d A(v+v_w)^2 v + (i/100)mgv$$

In the model and in the above equation, the impact of curve losses is missing. We have neglected this so far. It is nevertheless possible to add this to the model. In curves we experience a centripetal force F_{cp}, which depends on the body weight m, the curve radius r and the speed v:

$$F_{cp} = mv^2/r$$

This centripetal force provides an extra resistance and we must therefore use part of our running power to overcome this extra resistance. Consequently, in curves less of our power P is available for the "normal" resistances. The result is that we slow down in curves. How much we can estimate by comparing F_{cp} with the gravity force F_g:

$$F_{cp}/F_g = v^2/(r*g)$$

Next, we add the two forces (vector wise) and propose that the velocity decreases directly in proportion to the increase in force, in accordance with our running model. The figure below shows the result for curve radii of 5 meter (the minimum according to the IAAF), 17.5 meter (oval indoor track), 36.8 meter (oval outdoor track) and 100 meter and for 2 velocities (speeds), namely 5.86 m/s (2 hours Marathon) and 2.93 m/s (4 hours Marathon).

We see that the velocity reduction is limited and less than 1% at a curve radius of 37.8 m (corresponding to an oval outside track) or more.

Finally, we can calculate the time loss Δt of a 180° turn with the formula:

$$\Delta t = \pi r/v_b - \pi r/v$$

where v is the velocity on the straight and v_b is the (lower) velocity in the bend.

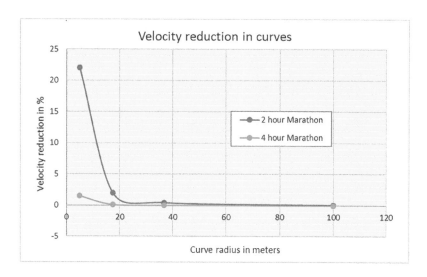

The resulting time loss is shown in the figure below.

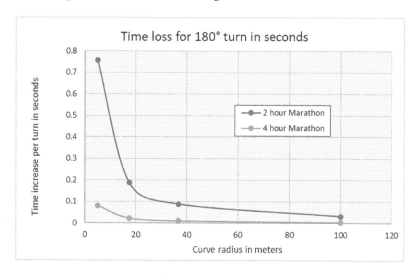

We see that the time loss of a 180° turn is very small. Even for Eliud Kipchoge, the time loss is less than 0.1 second for turns with a 37.8 m curve radius, corresponding to an oval outdoor track. For slower runners, the loss is even smaller.

Literature and data from practice
Two interesting papers on this topic were published by scientists involved in the INEOS 1:59 Challenge in Vienna.

In the first paper[1], the authors use a similar approach on the centripetal forces as above. However, they do not calculate the velocity decrease due to the centripetal forces based on our running power model. Based on literature, they assume that the metabolic energy use is related to the leg force F_b by a factor of $0.6234*F_b+0.3766$. Their results are comparable to ours, albeit that their time loss in the 180° turn is slightly smaller (a maximum of 0.26 seconds for tight curves). They also present an analysis of the Breaking 2 record attempt in Monza. They calculate that Eliud Kipchoge ran 71 curves with a total time loss of 1.52 seconds. This number is so low because the curves in Monza are wide, with curve radii between 23 m and 350 m. They also report that the marathon racecourse in Berlin has around 50 bends and the racecourse in London 70.

The second paper[2] provides a detailed analysis of the INEOS 1:59 race course in Vienna. There the lap only contained 2 wide curves (2 roundabouts with a curve radius of 23-135 m and 50-251 m respectively), and a total of 4 laps had to be run. They calculate that the total time loss in the 9 curves was limited to 0.49 seconds! They also calculate the time gain due to the fact that the first part of the course fell 13 meters (gain 6 seconds) and the time loss due to the elevation difference of 3 meters that Eliud had to overcome each round (loss 10.1 seconds).

Conclusion

The most important conclusion is that the time loss due to curves in the practice of the big city marathons is much smaller than is often perceived. Even at the speeds of world best runners, it is only a matter of seconds in total, while the loss among recreational runners is completely negligible.

It should be noted that this does not include the possible running of too many meters. Certainly in the hustle and bustle of recreational runners, this can easily lead to an additional half a km and therefore a loss of a few minutes!

With tight indoor tracks, the time loss is not entirely negligible. According to a calculation, the world record of 2:01:39 is equivalent to a time of 2:02:00 on an oval indoor track, so a 21 seconds difference due to the tight curves.

[1] Modeling the effect of curves on distance running performance, P. Taboga and R. Kram, https://doi.org/10.7287/peerj.preprints.27884v1
[2] The effects of course design (elevation undulations and curves) on marathon running performance: an a priori case study of the INEOS 1:59 Challenge in Vienna, C. Triska, W. Hoogkamer, K. Snyder, P. Taboga, C. Arellano and R. Kram, SportRxiv Preprints, https://doi.org/10.31236/osf.io/xrjvb

4.8 The energy cost of hills

The power required to overcome the climbing resistance depends on the gradient i (in %), the body weight m (in kg) and the speed v (in m/s), as shown in the box.

> ## The Climbing Resistance
>
> $P_c = (i/100)mgv$
>
> Example:
> i = 7.4%, m = 70 kg, v = 12.06 km/h, g = 9.81 m/s^2
> P_c = 7.4/100*70*9.81*12.06/3.6 = 170 watts

The example is valid again for the Marathon Man, who attempts to run to the top of the epic Alpe d'Huez in France. The numbers show that uphill he cannot maintain a speed of 12.06 km/h, as this would require a climbing resistance of 170 Watts on top of the 230 Watts that he needs for the running resistance and the 5 Watts for the air-resistance. So he will have to reduce his speed until the sum of the 3 resistances equals the power of his human engine (235 Watts for the Marathon Man).

In practice, it was found that the climbing resistance P_c is somewhat less than follows from the theoretical formula. This will be discussed in this chapter.

The hill factor

In literature it has been established that the climbing resistance is somewhat less than could be expected from theory. The difference is explained with the

The climb to Alpe d'Huez known from the Tour de France

muscle efficiency. According to physiology, the muscle efficiency is higher when positive work is executed (as in running uphill) and lower when negative work is done (as in running downhill).

The muscle efficiency can even be negative, at extreme downhill slopes when brake forces are dominant. We recalculated the oxygen demand to the specific power in Watts/kg, by using the fact that the energy value of 1 liter of O_2 is 19.5 kJ. Finally we have determined a hill factor η (in %) as the ratio of the measured power P and the theoretical required power P_k:

$\eta = P/P_k*100$

The results are given below:

Hill factor in literature	
	η in %
ACSM - running	39.6
ACSM - walking	79.3
Pugh - running	51.5
Pugh - walking	77.2
Davies - running	59.9
Davies - downhill	28.7

In spite of the different results, we see a consistent pattern. The hill factor and thus the required power is always less than 100%. Moreover, the hill factor is always less downhill than uphill. This means that the energy advantage of going downhill is always less than the disadvantage of going uphill. This is consistent with the explanation of a lower muscle efficiency downhill as a result of brake forces. Finally, the hill factor for running is always lower than it is for walking.

The research of Minetti et al.

The most convincing research in this field has been carried out by Minetti et al. They measured the energy cost of running up and down an extreme range of gradients, from -45% to +45%. We have calculated the hill factor equivalent to their results, see the figure.

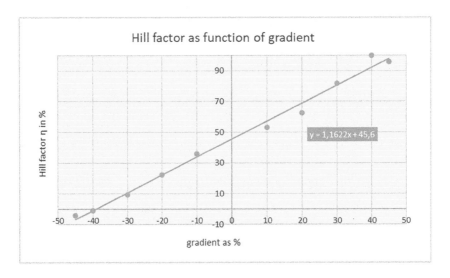

The results look reliable and reproducible. The hill factor is almost linearly dependent on the gradient. At extreme positive (uphill) gradients, the hill factor approaches 100%. At extreme negative (downhill) gradients, the hill factor even becomes negative! This means you have to use energy for braking without benefitting from the gain in altitude. We have concluded that these results are very useful, so we have included them in our running model, in accordance with the relationship of Minetti:

$$\eta = 45.6 + 1.1622i$$

The consequence is that the climbing resistance of the Marathon Man in the box is not 170 Watts, but only 170*(45.6+1.1622*8.1)/100 = 98 Watts.

Hoe large is the climbing resistance as a function of the gradient?

In the table below, we have calculated the climbing resistance (including the hill factor) for a speed of 15 km/h and as a function of the uphill gradient. The total climbing resistance obviously is proportional to the body weight, so the specific climbing resistance is actually a better parameter. In real life, many runners will not be able to maintain a speed of 15 km/h uphill, as the sum of the running resistance, the air-resistance and the climbing resistance will be larger than the available power of their human engine.

In the next chapter we explain *How much time do hills take?*.

Climbing resistance at 15 km/h			
Gradient	60 kg	70 kg	80 kg
i	P	P	P/m
(%)	(Watts)	(Watts)	(Watts)	(Watts/kg)
0	0	0	0	0.0
1	12	14	15	0.2
2	24	28	32	0.4
3	37	43	50	0.6
4	51	60	68	0.9
5	66	77	88	1.1
6	81	95	109	1.4
7	98	114	130	1.6
8	115	134	153	1.9
9	133	155	177	2.2
10	152	177	202	2.5
11	171	200	228	2.9
12	191	223	255	3.2
13	213	248	283	3.5
14	235	274	313	3.9
15	257	300	343	4.3
16	281	328	374	4.7
17	305	356	407	5.1
18	330	385	440	5.5
19	356	415	475	5.9
20	383	447	510	6.4
10.6	163	190	218	2.7

4.9 How much time do hills take?

In the battle for the fastest marathon course, you see that organizers do everything to eliminate undulations. Each meter up takes more energy than you recover down and means loss of time. This applies to all runners, recreational and elite.

World Athletics rule

For record attempts elevation differences are limited. Start and finish do not have to be exactly in the same place. This means that the finish may be lower than the start. That is beneficial for a fast time. To comply with the rules of World Athletics the difference in elevation between start and finish may not exceed 1 meter per km.

For example, the finish at the Boston Marathon is 140 meters lower than the start, which gives a theoretical advantage of about 3 minutes. This means that you can run faster than the world record here, but this will not be recognized.

In 2019 the start of the INEOS 1:59 Challenge of Eliud Kipchoge, who ran the marathon in 1:59:40.6, was in Vienna on top of the Reichsbrücke (bridge) over the river Danube. From there it went down 13 meters to the flat and straight route on the Hauptallee in the Prater park. This starting point was not only chosen because of its beautiful location. The elevation gain gave Kipchoge a push to get under 2 hours. However, other reasons made that Kipchoge's time in this orchestrated marathon could not be recognized as a world record.

The Running Model

For the evaluation of your running performance on a hilly course, you can use the formulas provided in earlier chapters. It is easier to assess the impact when

you enter the number of altimeters in the calculator on our website
www.theSecretofRunning.com.

State of the art is the Race Predictor from Stryd. Here you enter the GPX-file
of the course. The software then calculates your achievable time by taking the
full altitude profile of the course into account.

Recent literature

We have unraveled the secrets of running from theoretical laws of physics
and physiology and checked our findings in practice. If we see good practical
research, this triggers us to check whether we are right and whether we can
explain any differences.

For example, at the beginning of July 2021 we saw a new scientific publication by Marcel Lemire and others[1] on the impact of elevation differences. The
publication has been reviewed in advance by prof. Rodger Kram of Colorado
University in Boulder (USA). Kram was on the scientific team that supervised
Eliud Kipchoge's record attempts.

For diehards, we definitely recommend reading this article. For most people,
the figure below will suffice.

Lemire's findings

Marcel Lemire's research was conducted with 29 people, 10 women and 19
men. These individuals ran on a treadmill at different angles of inclination and
speeds. Partly on the basis of breathing gas analyses, all kinds of aspects of hill
running were investigated.

[1] Level, Uphill, and Downhill Running Economy Values Are Correlated Except on Steep Slopes,
Marcel Lemire et al, Frontiers in Physiology, July 2021, Volume 12, Article 697315, https://www.frontiersin.org/
articles/10.3389/fphys.2021.697315/full

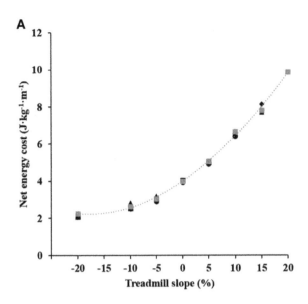

This resulted in, among other things, the figure above. You see that the energy consumption on a flat course (0%) is just over 4 kJ per kg body weight per kilometer. We recognize this. The rule of thumb of 1 kcal per kg body weight per km is well known. And 1 kcal equals 4.2 kJ.

For our books and articles, we use 1 kJ per kg per km in our running model on flat course. The muscle efficiency of elite athletes is 25%. So 1 kJ is used for running and 3 kJ is lost to heat that has to be dissipated by transpiration and running wind.

For less trained or talented runners, this efficiency can also be 23%. The 2% difference doesn't seem like much at first sight, but you have to consider that the impact on your running performance is 8.6% (25%/23% = 1.086). Compared to recreational runners the elite athletes get 8.6% more energy from their metabolism and are faster for just this reason.

In the figure you can see that an increasing gradient requires considerably more energy. In the event of a negative gradient, the energy consumption becomes less than on the flat, but by no way compensates for the extra energy consumption at the same gradient uphill.

For us, it confirms that these practical findings fit seamlessly with what we use in the running model.

Hill factor

In an earlier chapter we explained that the hill factor downhill is notable lower than uphill. That explains the shape of the graph in the figure below. This means that you benefit relatively less from energy gain downhill, which is in line with the loss of energy due to braking forces when descending.

With extreme slopes downhill, the hill factor even becomes negative. You then use so much energy to brake that you no longer benefit from the elevation gain.

In the figure below we show for Marathon Man what the impact of the slope percentage is on the running speed. Marathon Man runs the marathon in 3:30 and weighs 70 kg.

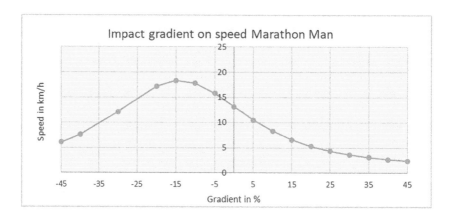

4.10 Wind from all directions

In augustus 2019 we tested the new Stryd with the revolutionary wind port for the first time in practice. This Stryd measures the air-resistance. Stryd calls this the 'Air Power'. The measuring device includes a 'wind port', a small hole at the bottom of the Stryd. A high-grade sensor measures the minute differences in air-pressure, comparable to the pitot-tube used in the aircraft industry.

We were lucky that Saturday. It was a windy day. By running back and forth on 2 tracks, we were able to get proper data of the Air Power from the Stryd. Stryd defines it as follows "Air Power represents the extra power needed to overcome air-resistance".

We found that the Stryd calculates realistic values, also in variable weather conditions. However, the results for tail winds did not match theory.

Experiences with daily use of the Stryd

We have used the Stryd daily on all of our workouts and races. Obviously, the weather conditions have been (very) different during all of these sessions.

With the restrictions mentioned the good news is that we found that the Air Power usually matched our theoretical calculations very well. Of course we were not able to measure the local wind speed and direction, so we had to rely on weather data. Also the wind is never constant, it changes upon the approach of rain clouds and in the wake of corn fields or trees. So we were not able to check the Air Power very accurately, but we can say that the data were always convincing, in the correct order of magnitude.

Wind correction Garmin Running Power

The Garmin Runnning Power IQ app for Garmin watches with barometer also include the impact of wind in the power calculation. You can turn wind correction on or off at the Garmin watch as desired. The watch needs te be connected to a smart phone in advance. Hereafter the watch takes the weather situation into account for power calculations. For changes occurring during your run the watch uses the barometric changes. We were not very enthusiastic about the results in our tests because it appeared not to be very precise.

The impact of the wind direction/angle

Earlier we explained our approach that the total running power P_t should be equal to the sum of the running resistance P_r and the air-resistance P_a on a flat course, so $P_t = P_r + P_a$.

P_r can be easily calculated. We know that Ron weighs 80 kg and has an ECOR of 1.04 kJ/kg/km at a pace of 5:45/km (speed 2.9 m/s). Consequently, his P_r is 1.04*2.9*80 = 241 Watts.

Obviously, P_a depends on the wind speed and direction. This is quite a complicated 6th order polynomial relationship, for which our running friend Arno Baels has prepared a spreadsheet calculator. The results are given in the figure below.

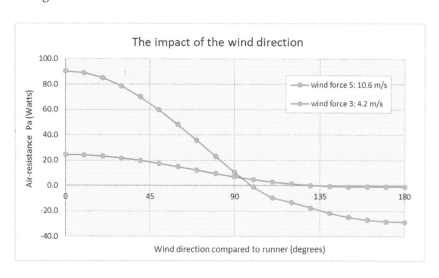

The green line gives the data for a wind speed of 38 km/h (wind force 5). These were the data of our first test on August 10, 2019. The figure shows that with a head wind P_a is as high as 90 Watts! At a cross wind (90 degrees) P_a is still 10 Watts, whereas with a tail wind P_a becomes -15 Watts. So with a tail wind, you are literally pushed by the wind.

The orange line gives the data for a wind speed of 15 km/h (wind force 3). These conditions occur regularly in the Netherlands, they might be considered average. In this case P_a is only 20 Watts facing a head wind. With a tail wind P_a is approximately 0.

Both in training and in races, you will probably experience variable wind directions as the course will never be a straight line. Part of the course you will enjoy a tail wind and part of the course you will have to battle against a head wind. Stryd PowerCenter presents the Air Power as a percentage of the total power so you are able to evaluate your performance.

The figure shows that the impact of the air-resistance at the lower wind speeds is around 5% of the total power, but a the higher wind speed (38 km/h), it increases to 20%!

4.11 How does the wind impact your 5K-race time?

W e frequently discuss the worldwide quest of runners, coaches and running scientists for options to optimize the running performance through reducing the air-resistance. Cyclists and speed-skaters have been doing this for a long time already by developing optimal aerodynamic conditions (clothing, frames, body position, streamlining, drafting).

In our columns at www.theSecretofRunning.com we discussed the development of the Stryd, which measures the Air Power in real time and the sensational INEOS 1:59 Challenge. In Vienna, Eliud Kipchoge was helped by 41 pacers (5 teams of 7 pacers and 6 reserves) to achieve his magnificent 1:59:40. We evaluated the impact of the huge fans providing tail wind that helped Justin Gatlin to run 9.45 seconds in the 100 meters. Both cases are described in separate chapters of this book.

In this chapter, we will calculate concretely and exactly how big the impact of the wind speed and the wind direction is on the running speed. As an example, we use author Hans, who weights 58 kg and can run a 5K-race time of 18 minutes (or at least he could, since he is currently injured).

Theory

According to the fundamental laws of physics, the power required to surmount the air-resistance P_a is determined by the density of the air ϱ (in kg/m^3) the air-resistance factor c_dA (in m^2), the running speed v (in m/s) and the wind speed v_w (in m/s), as:

$$P_a = 0.5 * \varrho * c_dA * (v+v_w)^2 * v$$

The figure below shows the air-resistance as a function of running speed v at the standard conditions (temperature 20°C, air-pressure 1013 mbar, so ρ = 1.205 kg/m³, c_dA = 0.24 m², no wind, so v_w = 0 m/s).

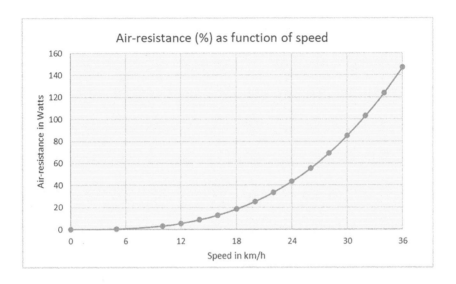

First, we assume that Hans ran his time of 18 minutes in ideal conditions, so no wind (v_w = 0). Consequently, his air-resistance P_a will have been equal to 14 Watts at the standard conditions and at his running speed of 5000/18/60 = 4.63 m/s. His running resistance P_r will have been equal to 4.63*58 (kg)*0.98 (ECOR in kJ/kg) = 263 Watts. So, his total power is equal to 263+14 = 277 Watts.

How big is the impact of the wind on the air-resistance P_a?

Next, we have calculated P_a at different wind speeds of 2, 8 and 16 m/s (58 km/h, hard wind force 7) and both for a head wind and a tail wind. The results are given in the figure below.

The head wind P_a increases from 14 Watts to no less than 131 Watts, which is almost half of the total power of 277 Watts of Hans.
At a tail wind P_a decreases from 14 Watts to finally -86 Watts (which means he literally gets a push in the back from the wind).

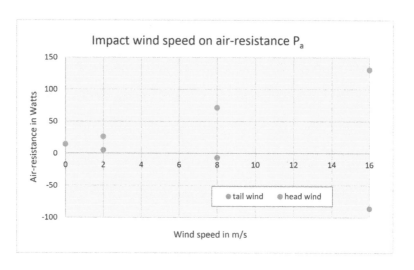

What is the impact on the 5K-race time?

We have calculated this from the power balance for a flat course: $P_t = P_a + P_r$. Earlier we saw that the P_t of Hans is 277 Watts. Consequently, his running power P_r decreases as P_a increases (head wind) and vice versa P_r increases as P_a decreases (tail wind). The resulting P_r is given in the figure below.

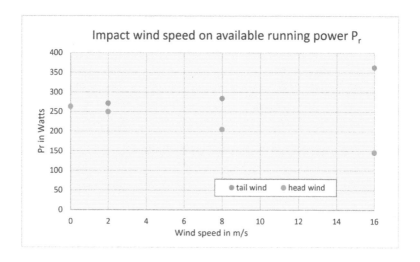

We notice that the available power P_r decreases significantly at a head wind (from 263 Watts to 146 Watts) and increases at a tail wind (from 263 Watts to 363 Watts).

Of course this has a big impact on the running speed, which can be determined with the formula v (in m/s) = P_r/58/0.98. Finally, we can calculate the 5K-race time t (in seconds) from the running speed with the formula t = 5000/v. The final result of the 5K-race time is given in the figure below.

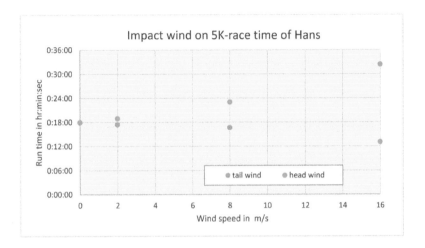

We see that the 5K-race time increases from 18 minutes to more than 32 minutes at a head wind of 16 m/s! With a tail wind of 16 m/s, the race time drops from 18 minutes to just over 13 minutes! If we could run races with a tail wind of 16 m/s, wow, what a PB could we get.....

And how about the impact of cross wind?

In real life we never experience a head wind or a tail wind during the whole race. So it is relevant to look at cross winds too. The formulas become more complicated in this case as we have to calculate with vectors of the wind direction and the running direction (the so-called apparent wind).

The result is a 6th order polynomial relationship. In the table below, we show the results for a wind speed of 16 m/s and various wind directions (angles).

The table clearly shows that the impact is huge at this wind speed. The air-resistance changes significantly at different wind angels and so does the 5K-race time!

Finally, we have calculated the impact on the 5K-race time of a hypothetical race

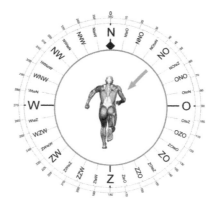

Impact of wind direction at wind speed 16 m/s (Wind force 7)	P_a (Watts)	P_r (Watts)	5K-time (min:sec)
head wind (0 degrees)	131	146	32:26
cross wind (45 degrees)	111	166	28:32
cross wind (90 degrees)	42	235	20:09
cross wind (135 degrees)	-59	336	14:06
tail wind (180 degrees)	-86	363	13:03

course with 1 km head wind, 1 km cross wind (45 degrees), 1 km cross wind (90 degrees), 1 km cross wind (135 degrees) and 1 km tail wind. This would lead to a race time of 21:39, so more than 3 minutes slower than at no wind.

We are lucky that Stryd can measure P_a these days!

We feel that the above calculations provide ample arguments to use a Stryd. At strong winds, P_a will have a big impact on the available running power P_r and resulting running speed.

Using a Stryd Hans can just maintain his total power P_t at 277 Watts. As a result his pace will automatically go up and down with the wind and he does not have to worry about over- or underpowering.

In an earlier chapter, we have shown that the Stryd can measure P_a accurately in head winds. In all honesty we have to say that the results at tail winds were not yet perfect, but we understand that Stryd is working hard to solve this part of the algorithm as well.

How big was the impact of the wind on your race time?

After a windy race, you can use the calculator on our website www.thesecretof-running.com to get an impression of the time that you could have run in ideal conditions (without wind). It is only an impression as we do not know whether the conditions were variable or you have been able to draft in a pack or in the wake of trees and buildings.

4.12 About your running efficiency

In one of the chapters in part V of this book we show how you can easily convert an existing training plan into a training plan based on power. The great thing is that you can personalize it if you know what your running efficiency is.

With the help of a running power meter, you can attach a value to your running efficiency. And if you have a value, you can use gait training to improve your running performance. This is not always easy. Habits are hard to change.

ECOR

The value we're talking about is the specific energy consumption, the amount of energy you need per kilogram of body weight to run a kilometer. The commonly used term is Energy Cost of Running (ECOR). The corresponding unit is kJ/kg/km.

A typical trained athlete who has had running training has an ECOR of 1.04 (including running wind, on a virtually windless day). Depending on the brand and model for the newest shoes the ECOR might be 4% less: 1.00 kJ/kg/km. A recreational runner may be at 1.10 or even higher, which means the runner uses relatively more energy to perform the same as the skilled athlete.

How do you know your ECOR?

If you want to know your ECOR exactly, it's good to check out a few results from your races or workouts at race pace. Take days with little wind, a flat and paved course, and distances in the order of 5 to 15K.

You calculate your ECOR from the average power and average pace at which you have run. If you take a few road races or fast time trials, you have a good indication of your personal running efficiency (which you might be able to improve through training).

An example for a 70 kg runner: you have averaged 250 Watts at an average pace of 4:53/km, i.e. 1000 meters in 293 seconds = 3.41 m/s.

You calculate the ECOR by dividing the wattage by your weight (250/70 = 3.57 Watts/kg) and by the running speed (3.57 Watts/kg)/(3.41 m/s) = ECOR 1,047 kJ/kg/km. Rounded 1.05.

If you do this calculation for several situations, you have a good indication of the personal value you can use instead of 1.04 in future.

Remember that if there are many elevation differences in the course, or if there is a strong wind, the ECOR is always higher. After all, it will cost you more energy to run at the same pace under these conditions. The ECOR is lower if you run in a group all the time. That is one of the reasons that Eliud Kipchoge could run the sub2 hours marathon in Vienna. It is also the reason that you have to determine your personal ECOR with no or little wind on a flat and paved course.

Does it matter 1.04 or 1.07?

This certainly matters. It means that with the same human power you can run a few percent faster. 3% difference for a marathon in 3:30 means about 6 minutes difference. If you do 4 hours on the marathon the difference is about 7.5 minutes.

Your personal human engine has a certain power. From the calculations earlier in this chapter you can conclude that you can keep a higher pace when you run more efficiently (with lower ECOR).

Furthermore, you see that your weight is important. If you gained weight after the seasonal holidays, the wattage drops per kg. At the same power, you'll run slower.

Measuring is knowing

You calculate your ECOR from your power data from fast training sessions and races over 5 to 15K on days with little wind, on a flat course with hard surface. When the wind blows and on a hilly course, running takes more energy. The calculated ECOR may be interesting, but is not suitable as a measure of your running efficiency.

The newest shoes can improve your running performance. Working on your running style and running efficiency can also be an option. Or both, of course.

ECOR and RE Relationship

Traditionally, runners know the concept of Running Efficiency (RE). Running Efficiency is defined as the specific oxygen consumption (in ml O_2/kg/km). It can be determine during a treadmill test at a sports medical advisory center. There is a fixed relationship between the specific energy consumption ECOR (in kJ/kg/km) and the specific oxygen consumption RE (in ml O_2/kg/km). The energy production of 1 ml O_2 is equal to 19.5 Joule and the muscle efficiency, 25% for elite athletes. An RE of 201 ml O_2/kg/km corresponds to an ECOR-value of 201*19.5*0.25/1000 = 0.98 kJ/kg/km.

This 0.98 is less than the ECOR 1.04 kJ/kg/km that we mentioned earlier. In the 1.04 the running wind is also included. The 0.98 applies to running on a level treadmill.

The ECOR and the RE are not the same for everyone and in all conditions, so it may deviate from 0.98 kJ/kg/km and 201 ml O_2/kg/km. There are many articles and books that describe that the RE may be lower or higher. Some marathon runners, especially Kenyans and Ethiopians, have a very efficient running style, which means that they consume less oxygen and therefore have a low RE and ECOR.

Metabolic efficiency

Together with the Radboud University in Nijmegen (the Netherlands), we have done practical research into the relationship between ECOR and RE. In that study, we found that untrained runners had a muscle efficiency (metabolic efficiency) of 23%. The trained runners were with 24% significantly more efficient. A metabolic efficiency difference of 1% means that when they run with the same power they needed 4% less oxygen than the untrained runners. Elite athletes have a muscle efficiency of 25% and therefore run even faster.

As an example we give the ECOR of the elite athletes on super shoes who assisted Eliud Kipchoge to run the marathon under 2 hours (Vienna 1:59:40): 0.93 kJ/kg/km. This is 5% better than 0.98!

In the chapter Super shoes you will learn that this is partly due to newly developed shoes.

With a running power meter with the accuracy of a Stryd, you can express your running efficiency in a number, the ECOR. And since you now know that ECOR has a direct relationship with the RE, you don't necessarily have to go to the exercise laboratory of a sports medical center anymore. And by regularly calculating your ECOR, you can now check for yourself whether your running training is paying out or not.

RE is also related to your physique

According to the literature, the running efficiency is determined by our physique and our running style. The theory of biomechanics shows the following factors for the physique:

• Weight of legs (light/slender lower legs are favorable)
• Lever Achilles tendon (small feet are beneficial)
• Leg length (long legs are beneficial)
• Hip angle (narrow and flexible hips are beneficial)

We cannot control these factors ourselves. At most, by losing weight, we can remove some excess fat from our legs and calves. However, we can try to get our joints, especially ankle, knee and hip, as flexible as possible through exercises and running training.

Running Style

The most concrete factor we can work on to improve running efficiency is the running style. This includes, for example, a short and springy ground contact, avoiding heel landing, using the arms to support the running movement and stretching the toes at the push-off. Runners do differ in opinion on what is the optimal running style with the highest efficiency. The factors that we can most easily influence ourselves are the cadence, the stride length and the vertical oscillation.

How much effect does ECOR have?

For this chapter, we calculated the potential effect of a higher or lower ECOR. In addition to the standard value of 1.04 kJ/kg/km (including running wind) we also took 2 alternatives:

1. a higher ECOR of 1.10 kJ/kg/km (this higher ECOR means that the runner consumes more energy and more oxygen and therefore runs less efficiently)
2. a lower ECOR of 1.00 kJ/kg/km (this is a low value that we see in the highly efficient elite athletes)

In the table below we show what this would mean for the achievable speed and duration of our Marathon Man who runs 3:30 on the marathon and weighs 70 kg. You can see the effect of the ECOR on the race times. For fast times it is important to run as efficiently as possible.

Effect ECOR Marathon Man			
Distance (km)	ECOR 1.04 (hr:min:sec)	ECOR 1.00 (hr:min:sec)	ECOR 1.10 (hr:min:sec)
1.5	0:05:59	0:05:45	0:06:20
3	0:12:32	0:12:03	0:13:15
5	0:21:36	0:20:46	0:22:51
10	0:45:13	0:43:29	0:47:50
15	1:09:41	1:07:00	1:13:42
20	1:34:42	1:31:04	1:40:10
21.1	1:40:16	1:36:25	1:46:03
25	2:00:09	1:55:32	2:07:05
30	2:25:57	2:20:20	2:34:22
42.195	3:30:00	3:21:56	3:42:07

4.13 Determine your FTP and your training zones

One of the advantages of power meters such as the Stryd is that you can determine your own Functional Threshold Power (your FTP, in Watts/kg). Your FTP corresponds to an effort that you can maintain for 1 hour. It is a very important parameter to predict your attainable speed and race time at various distances.

Before, you had to go to a test center to determine your FTP. With a running power meter, you can do it yourself and as frequently as you like. This means you can keep track how your fitness changes over time. The FTP is also important to determine your training zones, as we will explain in this chapter. You can easily adjust these zones when your FTP increases or decreases.

The Stryd Critical Power test

Like VO_2 max and FTP, Stryd's Critical Power (CP) is a benchmark of your fitness. It is a single value that tells you your fitness and whether your overall running fitness is increasing or decreasing. When normalized by weight, CP allows fair comparison between runners. Stryd defines the CP for runners as the threshold at which the dominant type of fatigue your body experiences changes. Typically, this is the duration of a 10K race for most runners. CP is therefore slightly different than your FTP (unless your 10K race time is one hour), which corresponds to the power which an athlete can maintain for 1 hour and also can be expressed as CP60.

The Stryd system automatically calculates your critical power. However, if you have doubt about the accuracy, you do a manual critical power test. While a manual test at a running track works best, you can also use an alternative measured course. Stryd's standard protocol for the track is as follows:

- Warm up 5 minutes.
- Easy pace run 800 m (2 laps).
- Easy run/warm up 5 minutes.
- Max-effort run 1200 m (3 laps).
- Recovery 30 minutes (walk/active recovery/easy running).
- Max-effort run 2400 m (6 laps).
- Cool down 10 minutes.

A manual test takes a snapshot of your fitness at a single point in time. Even though your fitness capabilities were constantly changing, your training zones would remain static until you completed another test. A valuable feature is the Stryd's ecosystem option to auto-calculate your CP from your recent training data. The auto-calculated CP will adapt your power zones to your changing fitness.

The manual test can be difficult to get right as for many runners it can be hard to truly run at maximum effort during a short duration. Another way to test (and increase if warranted) your CP is to do an all-out effort in the range 20 - 50 minutes. For many people this could be a 5K or 10K race, a fun way to test yourself. If you have automatic CP enabled, your CP will automatically increase if your run was harder than any previous workout in the last 90 days. If you use manual CP value, you can enter a 5K or 10K duration in the Stryd mobile app to manually calculate your CP and training zones.

The Polar watch test

Another example is Polar's Running Performance Test. Polar designed this tool especially for runners allowing them to track their progress and find out their unique training zones (heart rate, speed and power zones). By knowing your training zones, Polar provides individualized training guidance.

First the Polar watch asks to define your initial speed for the test. This is done in the Polar watch in Tests > Running test > Initial speed. The initial speed can be set between 4-10 min/km (default speed is 10 min/km).

Then go to Tests > Running test > Start and scroll down to see an overview of the test. When you're ready to start the test, choose Next. The test begins with a warming-up phase (10 minutes). After a proper warming-up, start the test. Then you need to reach the initial speed for the actual test to start.

During the test a blue value shows the steadily increasing target speed that should be followed as precisely as possible. A white value below shows your current speed. The watch gives an audible alarm if you go too fast or too slow.

When you're finished the watch will ask Was this your maximum effort? if the maximum heart rate value is not reached or is exceeded the test is considered submaximal if the effort wasn't maximal but at least 85 % of the maximum heart rate is reached. The test is automatically considered maximal, if you reach or exceed your current maximum heart rate value.

The Polar Running Performance Test gives a personal maximum aerobic power (MAP), maximum aerobic speed (MAS) and maximal oxygen uptake (VO$_2$ max) as results.

Note: be aware that power values determined with Polar and Garmin watches are higher than the values used in this book. For the backgrounds of this phenomena see the chapter Why native Polar (and Garmin) running power values are 25-30% too high?

A simple and science-based test

For those that cannot or do not want to use the Stryd or Polar system, we have developed an easy method. Our method is based on the physiological science of the time-power relationship as explained in this book. Remember that the FTP is the amount of power that you can maintain for 1 hour. Of course, it is not very practical to perform a test of 1 hour, as this would be too exhausting. But we know the power-time relationship, as we discussed in an earlier chapter.

Let's look at an all-out test of 10 minutes, the power output will obviously be higher than the FTP, by a factor of $(10/60)^{-0.07} = 1.13$. You can determine your FTP by dividing the specific power output during a 10-minute all-out test by the factor 1.13.

Such a test can be easily integrated in a training plan and is in fact a good workout. We recommend doing this test once every 6 to 8 weeks, so you keep track of your fitness and assess whether your progress as desired. The following protocol can be used:

• Warming-up 10 - 20 minutes (with some accelerations).
• Max-effort run 10 minutes
• Cooling-down 10 minutes

By repeating this test regularly, you will get a better grip of how your fitness and performance level evolve in time.

Determining your training zones

Now you have determined your FTP, you can determine your own training zones. Based on the literature and our own experience, we have compiled the following table, detailing 7 training zones to stimulate and improve the different energy systems of your human engine.

Note that some coaches have more power zones (more precise training) and some use fewer zones (easier for runners). Any number of zones can be helpful, and the number of zones is part of the personal preference.

Zone	Training goal	Training form	%F
0	Circulation in muscles	Warming up and recovery training	60
1	Improvement aerobic capacity and aerobic efficiency	Endurance training (10 - 30 km)	70
2	Improvement transition from aerobic to anaerobic system	Tempo endurance training with long tempo blocs (3 - 5 km)	80
3	Improvement lactate threshold power and anaerobic efficiency	Extensive interval training with longer blocs (1000 m)	90
4	Improvement lactate tolerance and VO$_2$ max	Intensive interval training with shorter blocs (400 m)	100
5	Improvement anaerobic capacity	Speed training (200 m intervals)	110
6	Improvement explosive power	Sprint training (50 - 100 m)	>>

Explanation

Zone 0: Active recovery

This zone includes warming up and easy runs with a duration of 30 - 90 minutes and an intensity of less than 70% of your FTP. The goal is to recover from previous hard training sessions or races. Warming up and cooling down are also part of this zone.

Zone 1: Endurance training

This zone includes both the short daily base runs (around 10 - 15 km) as well as the long weekly run (25 - 30 km). The intensity is 70 - 80% of your FTP. The goal is to stimulate and develop your muscles and aerobic capacity.

Zone 2: Tempo endurance training

This zone includes the higher intensity brisk tempo blocs (distances 3 - 5 km). The intensity is 80 - 90% of your FTP. The goal is to stimulate and develop the transition zone between the aerobic and anaerobic systems and your pace endurance.

Zone 3: FTP training

This zone comprises the longer interval sessions (800 - 1000 - 1200 meters, for example 5*1000 m). The goal is to stimulate and develop your FTP. The intensity is 90 - 100% of your FTP.

Zone 4: VO$_2$ max training

In this zone the shorter interval sessions are done (400 - 600 meters, for example 10*400). The goal is to stimulate and develop your VO$_2$ max. The intensity is 100 - 110% of your FTP.

Zone 5: Anaerobic capacity training

This zone consists of very short intensive intervals (200 meters, for example 10*200). The goal is to stimulate and develop your anaerobic capacity and speed. The intensity is 110 - 150% of your FTP.

Zone 6: Neuromuscular power

This zone includes the high-speed sprint sessions (50 - 100 meters). They can be done with a flying start. These sessions stress and develop the neuromuscular power. The intensity must be above 150% of your FTP.

With a running power meter you can easily determine your own FTP. You do not need to perform complicated tests at a physiological lab or with mobile breathing gas analysis equipment (ergo spirometry).

4.14 The power-time relationship

In order to calculate the performance at different distances, we first need to consider the power-time relationship. Everybody knows that marathon pace is less than a 5K pace. As pace is determined by power, this means that the power of the human engine apparently decreases as time increases. In this chapter, we will analyze this power-time relationship in detail. How can we calculate the power decline as a function of time? And what is the cause for this decline? We will show that the power-time relationship is actually determined by the 4 energy systems of the human engine that we discuss in the next chapter. We will see that as time increases gradually the fuel mix of the human engine changes, which explains the decline of power with time.

Pete Riegel's famous formula

The relationship between speed and distance was first investigated by Pete Riegel[1]. He was a mechanical engineer and marathon runner and as he put it himself 'nuts about numbers'. He compared his race times at various distances with the world records and concluded that the speed declined exponentially as a function of the distance. Both for his own times as well as for the world records he found the same exponential relationship. Pete Riegel's formula is simple and straightforward:

$$v_2/v_1 = (d_2/d_1)^{-0.07}$$

In his formula d represents the distance and v is the speed. So the formula says quite simply that as the distance increases by a factor of 2, the speed decreases by 5% ($2^{-0.07} = 0.95$).

---

[1] P. Riegel, Time predicting, Runner's World, August 1977, and P. Riegel, Athletic records and human endurance, American Scientist, 69, May-June 1981

Fatigue resistance

Pete Riegel's formula is very powerful and is used in many running calculators on the Internet. In Pete's papers and in literature by others, there has been some debate on the value of the exponent -0.07. Sometimes -0.06 or -0.08 is also mentioned. These differences are related to the fatigue resistance. A runner with a very good fatigue resistance will have an exponent of -0.06, so his speed will only decline 4% as the distance doubles. However, for most runners -0.07 is the most realistic number. This exponent is also valid for the world records of both men and women, as can be seen in the graph below.

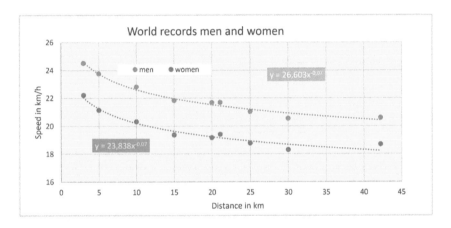

Both for men and women the data points are quite close to the regression line with an exponent $^{-0.07}$. As we will discuss later in this chapter, Riegel's formula works less well for short distances, so we have excluded these from the graph.

As the running power depends linearly on the speed (P_r = cmv), we can use Riegel's formula to describe the power-distance relationship as well. Apparently, we can conclude that as the distance doubles, the power decreases by 5% ($2^{-0.07}$ = 0.95) as well. As the distance is proportional with time, we can finally conclude that Riegel's formula can also be used to describe the power-time relationship.

How should we compare performances at different distances ?

In order to make an objective comparison of different performances, we should at least take into account the power-time relationship. A practical way of doing this, is by using Riegel's formula to make a table of the power-time relationship. As the base for the table, we chose the power that can be maintained for 1 hour.

We know from literature and experience that at this level the human engine is fueled virtually completely by the 2 aerobic energy systems, the aerobic conversion of glycogen and the aerobic conversion of fatty acids. These are the 2 primary energy systems for endurance sports. This level is called the Functional Threshold Power or FTP (in Watts/kg). The term threshold is used because at this level the anaerobic systems start to kick in.

The maximum FTP of male world champions in various sports is around 6.4 Watts/kg. We consider an FTP of 6.4 Watts/kg the ultimate limit of the human performance for men. For women it is 5.7 Watts/kg.

However, the FTP is not the maximum power output of the human engine. During a short period, everybody can mobilize more power than his FTP (as the FTP can be maintained for 1 hour). If you have to run for 10 minutes only, you can mobilize more power, i.e. $(10/60)^{-0.07}*100 = 113\%$ of your FTP. This means that during 10 minutes you can also run at a 13% higher speed than during 1 hour. The power-time relationship is given in the table.

Power ratio with time	
Time (minutes)	% FTP (%)
10 (= VO$_2$ max)	113
20	108
40	103
60 (= FTP)	100
120	95
240	91
300	89

We have set the lower limit of the table at 10 minutes, as during shorter times the anaerobic energy systems (the glycolysis and the conversion of ATP) become too important to be neglected. The available power (in Watts/kg) that can be maintained during 10 minutes is linearly proportional to the maximum oxygen uptake capacity, the VO_2 max. The table thus shows that the available power at the VO_2 max (duration 10 minutes) is 13% greater than at the power at the FTP (duration 60 minutes).

Contrary, we can say that the available power at the FTP is 100/113 = 88% of the power at the VO_2 max. Another well-known example is that the available power during 2 hours (which is nearly the approximate marathon time for world class runners) is equal to 95/113 = 84% of the VO_2 max. As the pace depends linearly on power, this means that world class athletes can run the marathon at approximately 84% of the pace at their VO_2 max.

What causes the decline of power with time?

From literature it is well-known that the ratio of the aerobic conversion of glycogen and the aerobic conversion of fatty acids (i.e. the 'fuel mix') is not constant. During rest, the fuel mix consists primarily of fatty acids. When we start running, the share of glycogen in the fuel mix increases rapidly. At the pace of the VO_2 max, the share of glycogen has increased to 90%. The figure on the next page shows experimental findings on the relationship between the exercise intensity and the fuel mix. Looking at the figure, you could also say that as you reduce your pace the share of the fatty acids in the fuel mix increases.

We wondered whether this could be the cause of the decline of power with time as expressed by Riegel's formula? To answer this question, we need to study the biochemistry of the human engine in some detail. That is done in the next chapter.

Conclusions on the power-time relationship

We conclude that the power-time relationship is expressed accurately by Riegel's formula, for time periods of 10 minutes and above. For most runners and for the world records in athletics, an exponent of -0.07 best describes the results at different distances. The decline in power with time as expressed by

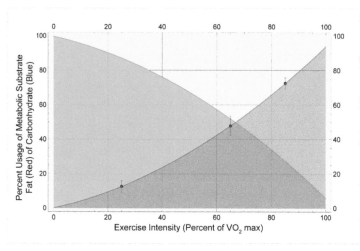

Fuel mix in muscles according to Rapoport[2]

Riegel's formula, can be explained by the change in fuel mix. At the marathon, the pace is slower than at 5K, so the muscles automatically use a fuel mix with more fatty acids.

For time periods shorter than 10 minutes, the pace and the available power is higher than described by Riegel's formula. This is caused by the increasing share of the anaerobic systems in the fuel mix. Unfortunately, only limited experimental findings are available on this. We have calculated that the maximal available power is 385% of the FTP during a short burst, like the 100 meters sprint.

Finally, we note that some deviations from the exponent of -0.07 can occur in practice, in particular for:
• Sprinters with a limited fatigue resistance (in this case the factor can be -0.08 or -0.09)
• Ultra-runners with exceptional fatigue resistance (in this case the factor can be -0.06 or -0.05)

[2] B.I. Rapoport, Metabolic factors limiting performance in marathon runners, PLoS Comput Biol 6 (10): e1000960, doi:10.1371/journal.pcbi.100960

4.15 Your four energy systems

So far, we have calculated a lot with the FTP, the specific power (in Watts/kg) that you can maintain for 1 hour. We have shown the FTP provides a good base to compare performances in different conditions and in different sports. Furthermore, we saw that the ultimate limit of human power can be set at an FTP of 6.40 Watts/kg for men and 5.70 Watts/kg for women.

Now we want to look more closely to the maximum limit of human power for performances with a different time-span, from short explosions in sprinting to protractive endurance power.

How big is the maximum power of the 4 energy systems?

In the table on the next page the biochemical limits of the specific power (in Watts/kg) are given of the 4 energy systems of the human engine. We note that we have prepared this table with data from the (thermodynamic/biochemical) literature, using the muscle efficiency of 25% and an (athletic) body weight for a world class athlete of 60 kg.

The table clearly shows that the maximum power is very different for the 4 systems. On the one hand, the ATP/PC system (Adenosine Triphosphate–Creatine Phosphate System) can supply a lot of power, but it can only sustain this for a brief explosion (10-15 seconds) like the 100 meters sprint (high power short duration). The ATP-PC is anaerobic because it doesn't require oxygen to function. ATP is short for adenosine triphosphate and ADP is adenosine diphosphate.

On the other hand, the conversion of fatty acids supplies much less power, but it can maintain this for a very long time (low power, long duration; many hours, even days).

Power output of the four fuels in the human engine	P/m (Watts/kg)
Anaerobic phosphogen system ATP/CP	
ATP → ADP $\quad C_{10}H_{16}N_5O_{13}P_3 \rightarrow C_{10}H_{15}N_5O_{10}P_2$	24.64
Anaerobic conversion of glycogen	
$C_6H_{12}O_6 + 3ADP \rightarrow 2C_3H_6O_3 + 3ATP$	13.50
Aerobic conversion of glycogen	
$C_6H_{12}O_6 + 6O_2 + 38ADP \rightarrow 6CO_2 + 6H_2O + 38ATP$	7.76
Aerobic conversion of fatty acids	
$CH_3(CH_2)_{14}COOH + 23O_2 + 130ADP \rightarrow 16CO_2 + 16H_2O + 130ATP$	2.36

Which fuel mix is used by sprinters and distance runners?

The human engine more or less automatically adapts the fuel mix. In rest and at relative low exercise intensity, mainly fatty acids are used. As more power is required, so at a higher pace in running, more and more glycogen is used in the fuel mix. At intensities above the FTP, the anaerobic breakdown of glycogen starts to kick in. Finally, near full (sprinting) power, ATP becomes the main fuel in the mix.

Obviously, you cannot maintain high paces for a long time, so the fuel mix depends also on the duration. Sprinters use mainly ATP and distance runners rely on a mix of glycogen and fatty acids. The gradual change in the fuel mix is

Fuel mix				
Time (minutes)	Anaerobic ATP (%)	Anaerobic Glycolysis (%)	Aerobic Glycogen (%)	Aerobic Fatty acids (%)
0	100	0	0	0
1	10	65	20	5
5	2	8	80	10
10	0	0	90	10
20	0	0	84	16
40	0	0	78	22
60	0	0	75	25
120	0	0	69	31
240	0	0	64	36

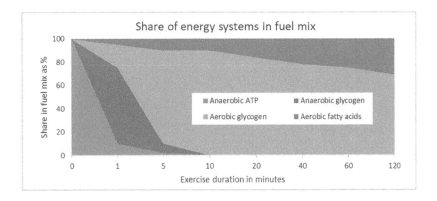

the reason for the gradual decline of power with time, as described by Riegel's formula in the previous chapter. The table and figure above summarize the composition of the fuel mix as a function of the time in minutes.

Limits of human power	
Time (minuten)	Specific power (Watts/kg)
0	24.64
1	12.91
5	8.02
10	7.22
20	6.90
40	6.57
60	6.41
120	6.09
240	5.82

How big is the maximum human power as a function of time?

When we multiply the share of the 4 energy systems with the specific power from the first table, we can calculate the maximum human power as a function of time. The result is given in the table and in the figure on the next page.

Can these limits be confirmed in the real world?

Earlier, we stated that the maximum level of the FTP (so the specific power that can be maintained for 1 hour) is indeed 6.4 Watts/kg for elite male athletes. This value is corroborated by the Power Profiles in cycling and we also found that the current world records in athletics are equivalent to these FTP's.

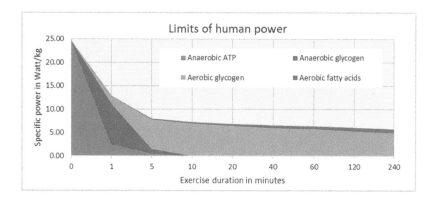

We have also calculated the specific power for other times than 1 hour. The table gives the results of our calculations on various world records. Almost all calculated power values are based on our model, which is based on the equilibrium situation, so without the power required to accelerate from the start.

The exceptions in the table are the data on the 100 - 400 meters, where we obviously had to include the additional power for the acceleration from 0 to 10 m/s during the first 4 seconds from the start. This is equivalent to an acceleration of 2.5 m/s$_2$. This acceleration requires an additional power (P/m = av) of 25 Watts/kg. As the acceleration lasts only 4 seconds, the impact on the average power of Usain Bolt is 4/9.58*25 = 10.5 Watts/kg. We have added this value to the equilibrium power of 12.0 Watts/kg. For Michael Johnson the average acceleration power comes down to 4/43*25 = 2.3 Watts/kg, which we have added to his equilibrium power of 10.6 Watts/kg. All in all the results of all the calculations match the theoretical limits very well.

Relevant Performances and Equivalent Powers	
Time (minutes)	Close examples
0	100 m 22.5 Watts/kg
1	400 m, 12.9 Watts/kg
5	3000 m, 7.32 Watts/kg
10	5000 m, 7.06 Watts/kg
20	10,000 m, 6.74 Watts/kg
40	15K, 6.41 Watts/kg
60	21.1 km, 6.36 Watts/kg
120	42.2 km, 5.99 Watts/kg

In summary, we conclude that the limits of human power can be based on the biochemical maximum values of the power of the 4 energy systems. The result is that the maximum power for a short explosion such as the 100 meters sprint is 24.6 Watts/kg. The maximum power that can be maintained for 1 hour (the FTP) is 6.4 Watts/kg. These data are confirmed by our analysis of the performances of elite athletes in running, cycling and ice-skating. The values are valid for male athletes, the values for women are some 11% lower, so at 5.7 Watts/kg. This difference is caused by the higher body fat percentage and the lower muscle power of women.

4.16 How big is the impact of the temperature?

We are impressed with Stryd's Race Calculator. Ron experienced the prediction of the temperature impact by this calculator in the 2021 Berlin Marathon. It was hot in Berlin which caused many runners to run a lesser time, including Kenenisa Bekele (2:06:47 versus 2:01:41 in 2019, so 4% slower).

We noticed in the evaluation of Berlin that Stryd's Race Power Calculator does not fully reflect the temperature effect for others than elite athletes, nor does it distinguish between lightweight and heavyweight runners. Earlier, we also saw that the Race Power Calculator for shorter distances than the marathon was not quite right either. We informed Stryd about our findings. In our experience, Stryd includes contributions like this in the further development of their ecosystem, as they call the features offered by this running power meter.

For this chapter, we have therefore listed all the information about the impact of temperature, distance and bodyweight on the performance loss in the heat, both for our readers and for the programmers of Stryd.

What is the optimum temperature?

All long distance runners have experienced such an ideal race: fast course, nice and flat, windless weather, nice group of runners and an ideal temperature. But what exactly is that, the ideal temperature?

The impact of the temperature on the performance in running is determined in practice by at least 2 factors:

1. At too low a temperature, we are forced to put on extra clothes to prevent us from suffering from the cold and our body from cooling down

too much. Extra clothing leads to extra weight and hinders our freedom of movement.

2. If the temperature is too high, we have problems getting rid of the heat that we produce ourselves when running and we run the risk of overheating and dehydration due to the sweat loss.

In practice, it appears that the optimal marathon temperature (in windless and dry weather) for the world class runners is somewhere near 5-10°C. You have to keep in mind that they produce more heat than recreational runners, so that for ordinary runners the optimum will be at 10-15°C. This is cool enough to get no problems with warming up and needs no extra clothes to be kept warm. Please note that wind and rain can lead to hypothermia and performance loss as well!

What effect does a high temperature have on our body?

We must distinguish between the effect of increasing the temperature of our body (hyperthermia) and the effect of dehydration.

When we run we produce more heat than we consume. We use no more than 23-25% of the energy to run. The rest is released as heat. This causes our body temperature to rise and we start sweating, to get rid of the heat.

At a low temperature, a lot of heat can already be dissipated by convection, so we have to sweat less. We cool down sufficiently by the air that flows past us while running. At a high air temperature, we sweat much more and the danger of dehydration threatens. With a combination of high air temperature and high humidity, we can hardly lose our heat anymore and the danger of heat stroke or collapse emerges.

The increase in body temperature has the important consequence that the blood vessels in our skin dilate, so that more blood flows to the skin and less blood is available for other functions, including our (leg) muscles. So our cardiovascular capacity is actually getting lower; if we run with a heart rate monitor, we notice this from the 'cardiac drift', that is, we run less fast with the same heart rate (HR) or get a higher HR at the same running speed.

The loss of sweat has the effect, among other things, that our blood volume decreases and the blood thickens, which further reduces the capacity of the heart and our performance. Eventually, the pressure in the veins can drop so much that the filling of the ventricle is compromised, forcing the HR to go up even further. If the body temperature rises above 39.5°C, the symptoms of heat stroke may occur (fainting, extreme fatigue, reduced ability to sweat).

Temperature influence at the marathon

Various studies have been reported in the literature in which the statistical relationship between the temperature and the realized times in the marathon has been examined. The best study is that of Helou et al[1]. They analyzed the results of more than 1.7 million participants in the Berlin, Boston, Chicago, London, New York and Paris marathons between 2001 and 2010.

They found a statistically significant relationship between the race times and the temperature, see the figure. They concluded that the performance loss among elite runners (P1) was less than among lesser runners (referred to as Q1, the fastest 25%, the median and Q3, the fastest 50-75%).

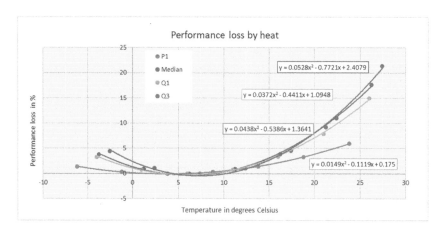

The results can be summarized as follows:
- The optimum temperature is about 5°C (world class runners 4°C, recreational runners 7°C)
- In the heat (25°C) the speed of elite runners is 6% lower and of recreational runners 12-18%

[1] Impact of Environmental Parameters on Marathon Running Performance, Nour El Helou et al., https://journals.plos.org/plosone/article?id=10.1371/journal.pone.0037407

• In women, the optimal temperature is a bit higher (9°C) and the speed loss is somewhat smaller (13% at 27°C). Women therefore suffer less from the heat.

These results are well in line with the previous study by Ely et al[2] that related the performance loss to the wet bulb temperature (which is always somewhat lower than the normal temperature), see the indicative table below:

Performance loss (in %) at 22°C i.r.t. 8°C	
Elite men	4.3
Elite women	5.6
25^e position	6.8
50^e position	8.6
100^e position	11.1
300^e position	21.0

What is the impact of body weight?

Tim Noakes, the author of 'The Lore of Running', summed up the impact of the loss of sweat on performance with the slogan 'all great marathoners are small'.

In the book The Secret of Running we showed that this is related to the fact that larger and heavier runners produce more heat and therefore have to produce more sweat to dissipate their heat. The most famous example of this is the Atlanta Olympic Marathon in 1996, which was run under tropical conditions at a temperature of 25°C and a relative humidity of 70%. Many runners suffered from the heat and the race was eventually won by South African lightweight Josiah Thugwane (43 kg), ahead of South Korean lightweight Lee Bon Ju (45 kg). We calculated that these lightweight runners produced 'only' 3.3 liters of sweat, against 10 liters for a runner of 90 kg!

If we look at the figure of Helou et al. with this knowledge, it is obvious to conclude that the lower performance loss of elite runners compared to recreational runners will in large part be related to the fact that most elite runners are small and lightweight. Roughly speaking, we dare to say that the performance loss will be proportional to the weight of the runner. Where an elite runner of 56 kg has a performance loss of 3%, Ron (80 kg) has to count with a

[2] Impact of weather on marathon-running performance, Matthew R Ely, et al., https://pubmed.ncbi.nlm.nih.gov/17473775/

performance loss of 4.3%. In addition to the bodyweight, the talent also plays a role: slower runners are longer on the road and will therefore suffer relatively more from the heat.

What is the optimum temperature at other distances?

It goes without saying that the impact of the temperature will be the biggest on the marathon distance. After all, at a shorter distance you will suffer less from warming. Also, it is known that sprinters in particular thrive best at higher temperatures. Their muscles must be sufficiently warmed up to be able to deliver maximum power for a short period of time. What the optimal temperature is at different distances has been investigated in another study[3]. The results are given in the table and graph below.

Optimum temperature		
Distance (km)	Men (°C)	Women (°C)
0.1	22.1	23.0
0.2	22.6	22.3
0.4	20.8	17.7
0.8	19.0	18.4
1.5	22.2	19.4
5	18.3	17.2
10	16.8	19.0
21.1	14.3	13.4
42.195	9.7	11.0

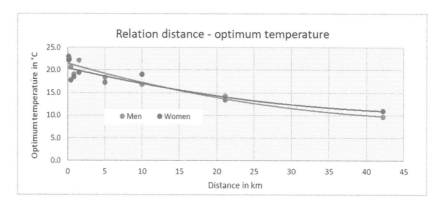

[3] Will le Page, Optimum temperature for elite running performance

The relationship from this figure makes a lot of sense. At the short distance, your muscles benefit from warm weather and you do not suffer from warming up. On the long distance it is becoming increasingly important that you can lose the heat you produce to the air and therefore a lower temperature is better. If the temperature is too low, you can suffer from hypothermia. This plays a major role, especially in wind and rain.

How big is the impact of the temperature at different distances?

We have not been able to find a good paper with concrete results on the impact of temperature at distances other than the marathon. Nevertheless, after some puzzling, we managed to deduce a relationship ourselves for the loss of time at different distances compared to the loss in the marathon, see the figure below.

We have based this on the study of Helou et al. for the marathon and the following additional considerations:

• The influence of the distance will be more than proportional; at the half marathon the effect is clearly less than half of the impact at the marathon.
• The influence will be minimal at very short distances; we have assumed that at 3000 meters the loss of time is negligible

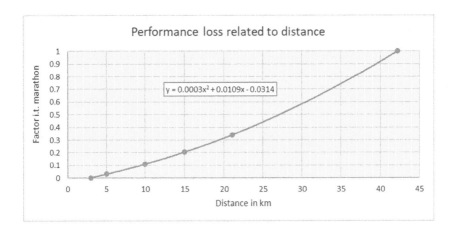

With the considerations in this chapter we hope to contribute to a correct estimate of the impact of the temperature, bodyweight and distance on the performance loss in the heat.

4.17 Super shoes

Ja, dit is de eerste keer dat ik er op loop en ik denk dat ze mij geholpen hebben.

Letensebet Gidey (2019): "Yes, this is the first time I have run on them and I think they have helped me."

We received the following interesting question from one of our fans, namely Eddie:

"I am happy to read your articles. Read some articles about running power meters and the Nike Vaporfly. The Vaporfly is about 4% more efficient than a regular shoe. I myself use the Asics Nimbus. My FTP is 324 Watts. I also have the Vaporfly and I want to use it for the first time for a fast 10K. According to your theory I can run this 10K with a power of 322 and I'll finish in 41:30. My question is: what is the impact of Vaporfly on power? Do I run with the same power faster on the Vaporfly or can I run on a higher power? If it is the last, can I add 4% to my FTP?"

We have informed Eddie that the FTP reflects the power of his human engine and therefore does NOT get higher if you wear fast super shoes. However, the power from a running power meter is not a direct measurement but calculated by an algorithm. This means that Eddie does have to add 4% to the 322 Watts. So he has to run his fast 10K at the power of 335 Watts. Because the energy consumption with the Vaporfly is up to 4% lower he will run about 3-4% faster than 41:30!

The power of your human engine doesn't get better with those new shoes. The crux is in the running economy. With a better running economy, you run more economically. Compare it to a car engine that is more fuel efficient. You run longer with your tank. You notice this by a lower heart rate at your paces. If you run with the same heart rate as usual you are faster (and your tank is not empty sooner).

Eddie's question did encourage us to review the current knowledge and literature about the impact of running shoes on race times. In this chapter, we will provide an overview of the energy consumption in running and the factors that influence this, including the recent development of carbon-plate shoes, such as the Nike Vaporfly. A lower ECOR means that you use less energy and can run faster with the same power.

How high is the energy consumption in running?

In our book The Secret of Running, we have included the following table on the specific energy consumption when running on a hard surface (ECOR in kJ/kg/km).

Specific energy cost of running and Running economy in literature		
ECOR (kJ/kg/km)	ECOR (kJ/kg/km)	RE (ml O_2/kg/km)
HGVH **1.000**	1.046	214
ACSM **0.934**	0.977	200
Sherman **0.897**	0.938	192
Slawinski 0.897	0.938	**192**
Zamparo 1.056	**1.104**	226
Sassi 0.961	**1.005**	206
Vroemen 0.841	0.879	**180**
Léger **0.980**	1.025	210
Léger **0.927**	0.970	198
Model value 0.938	0.981	201

When we consider that various authors have used different methods and the circumstances have also been different, it is remarkable that all values are close to the average. We concluded in The Secret of Running that it is very realistic to use the calculation value of 0,981 kJ/kg/km. This value has now become the universal standard and is also used by Stryd and other authors.

Is the energy consumption the same for everyone?

The specific energy consumption is NOT the same for everyone and under all circumstances. For example, it is well known that some marathon runners, especially the Kenyans and Ethiopians, have a high running efficiency. The running efficiency covers many aspects, the influence of which are not explicitly known. These include:
1. length (small is better)
2. physique (long legs, narrow calves, narrow and flexible hips are better)
3. running style:
    - foot landing (short ground contact, not on heel)
    - arm swing (not in front)
    - stride length and cadence (large strides high frequency)
    - vertical oscillation (effect not uncontroversial)

With the arrival of running power meters, it has become possible to easily measure your individual energy consumption by dividing your specific power (Watts/kg) from a training or race by your speed (in m/s): the result of the division is your ECOR in kJ/kg/km. Please note that you must correct – even in windless weather – for the power needed to overcome the air-resistance. This part is virtually negligible at low speeds, but with world class athletes it can be 7% or more.

How do your shoes affect your specific energy consumption?

It has traditionally been known that light shoes have an advantage: in The Secret of Running we have calculated that 100 grams of weight loss provides an advantage of 0.25-1.00%. Most race shoes are therefore already very light nowadays, in the order of 200 grams.

It was also known from the literature that shoes that use an air-bag and thermoplastic polyurethane foam (such as the Adidas BOOST) can reduce the ECOR by order by 1% because the foam is viscoelastic and returns part of the landing energy. The function of carbon shoes such as the Nike Vaporfly has been described by

Wouter Hoogkamer et al[1]. The secret of these shoes is twofold:
1. they use a carbon plate that functions like a spring
2. they use multiple layers of viscoelasticpolymers (PEBA) with a thickness of 40 mm.

(40 mm complies to the international athletic shoe regulations of World Athletics for road events, effective from 1 January 2022)

Hoogkamer measured in the laboratory that the Vaporfly's spring operation was able to return 7.46 Joule of energy per step compared to 3.38 J for the Nike Zoom Streak and 3.56 J for the Adidas BOOST2. If we divide the difference of 4 J/step for a world class athlete with a stride length of 1.5 m by 666 steps/km and a body weight of 60 kg, we come to a reduction of the ECOR of 0.04 kJ/kg/km. This exactly matches the 4% lower energy consumption that Nike claims!

By the way, the height of 40 mm also provides an advantage because the length of the lower leg increases slightly, as it were, which also has a positive effect on the running efficiency. Several studies have also shown that the stride length with the Vaporfly increases slightly (partly due to the spring action and partly due to the height), which also has a positive effect.

What effect do the new shoes have on the running time?

The new shoes have clearly led to an avalanche of records. The most famous is of course the phenomenal race of Eliud Kipchoge with his 1:59:40 in the INEOS 1:59 Challenge at 12 October 2019 (ran on Nike Alphafly shoes). The next day Bridget Koskei (also on Nike Alphafly) beat Paula Radcliffe's 16-year-old marathon world record to 2:14:04. A paper by Borja Muniz-Pardos et al[2]. shows that since the introduction of the Carbon shoes almost all world records have been improved on these shoes.

In the tables below we have listed how many % the world records have improved since the introduction of the newly developed shoes for track and road. The percentage still seems modest (at least compared to the 4% lower energy consumption) but it should be born in mind that the conditions will not have been ideal everywhere and the level of some old world records was very high

[1] A Comparison of the Energetic Cost of Running in Marathon Racing Shoes, Wouter Hoogkamer et al., Sports Medicine (2018) 48:1009–1019, https://link.springer.com/article/10.1007%2Fs40279-017-0811-2
[2] Recent Improvements in Marathon Run Times Are Likely Technological, Not Physiological, Borja Muniz-Pardos et al., Sports Medicine (2021) 51:371–378, https://link.springer.com/article/10.1007%2Fs40279-020-01420-7

| World Records: Men | | | | | |
Distance	Time 2017	Name	Time 2021	Name	faster
5,000 m	12:37.35	Kenenisa Bekele	12:35.36	Joshua Cheptegei	0.26%
10,000 m	26:17.53	Kenenisa Bekele	26:11.00	Joshua Cheptegei	0.41%
15 km	0:41:13	Leonard Komon	0:41:05	Joshua Cheptegei	0.32%
20 km	0:55:21	Zersenay Tadese	0:55:21	Zersenay Tadese	0.00%
21.1 km	0:58:23	Zersenay Tadese	0:57:31	Jacob Kiplimo	1.48%
25 km	1:11:18	Dennis Kimetto	1:11:18	Dennis Kimetto	0.00%
30 km	1:27:38	Emmanuel Mutai	1:26:45	Eliud Kipchoge	1.01%
42.2 km	2:02:57	Dennis Kimetto	2:01:39	Eliud Kipchoge	1.06%

| World Records: Women | | | | | |
Distance	Time 2017	Name	Time 2021	Name	faster
5,000 m	14:11.15	Tirunesh Dibaba	14:06.62	Letesenbet Gidey	0.53%
10,000 m	29:17.45	Almaz Ayana	29:01.03	Letesenbet Gidey	0.93%
15 km	0:46:14	Florence Kiplagat	0:44:20	Letesenbet Gidey	4.11%
20 km	1:01:54	Florence Kiplagat	1:01:25	Joyciline Jepkosgei	0.78%
21.1 km	1:04:52	Joyciline Jepkosgei	1:02:25	Letesenbet Gidey	3.78%
25 km	1:19:53	Mary Keitany	1:19:53	Mary Keitany	0.00%
30 km	1:38:49	Mizuki Noguchi	1:38:49	Mizuki Noguchi	0.00%
42.2 km	2:15:25	Paula Radcliffe	2:14:04	Brigid Kosgei	1.00%

(such as those of Kenenisa Bekele and Paula Radcliffe, who were clearly a class apart in their time). It is also illustrative of the latter that Bridget Koskei only improved Paula Radcliffe's world record by 1%, but her own PB by more than 3%. It should be noted that a 4% lower ECOR value theoretically corresponds to a slightly lower time saving of 3.4% due to the impact of air resistance.

Recent studies on time gains with carbon shoes

We refer to 5 interesting studies that have been published on the time gains from carbon shoes:

1.   *The World Athletics Report*[3]

They have made an analysis of the best season times of the top 20 and the top 100 runners for the 10 km, half marathon and the marathon. They conclude that since the introduction of carbon shoes in 2017, the race times have clearly improved (0.6-1.5% in men and 1.7-2.3% in women)

2.   *The Cornell Report*[4]

They analyzed the results of 22 North American marathons from 2015 to 2019. The special thing about this study is that they used thousands of web photos and video

[3] Effect of Advanced Shoe Technology on the Evolution of Road Race Times in Male and Female Elite Runners, https://www.frontiersin.org/articles/10.3389/fspor.2021.653173/full
[4] An Observational Study of the Effect of Nike Vaporfly Shoes on Marathon Performance, https://arxiv.org/pdf/2002.06105.pdf

recordings to determine which shoes the individual participants used. They concluded a benefit from carbon shoes of 1.4-2.8% for men and 0.6-2.2% for women.

3. The New York Times Report[5]

This is by far the most comprehensive study. They looked at the results of 577,000 marathons and 496,000 half marathons in dozens of countries from April 2014 to December 2019. They investigated the effect of the shoes in 4 ways: with statistical models, by looking at groups of runners who ran the same race, by looking at runners who had changed shoes and by looking at the chance to run a PB in a certain type of shoes. The results of the runners who switched shoes show an impressive advantage of the Vaporfly of even more than 4%! See the figure below (source: New York Times)

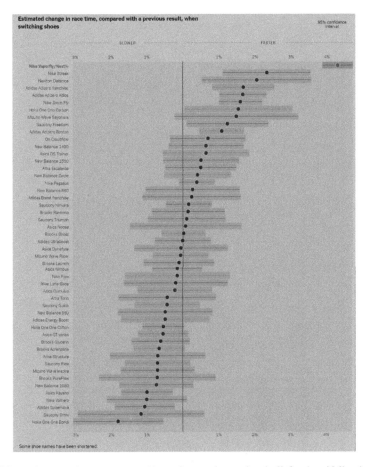

[5] Nike's fastest shoes may give runners an even bigger advantage than we thought, K. Quealy and J. Katz, https://www.nytimes.com/interactive/2019/12/13/upshot/nike-vaporfly-next-percent-shoe-estimates.html

4. Hechmann's research[6]

This is a very special case: a solo study by a passionate Danish researcher. Hechmann used ten pairs of different shoes in different weight classes. He used a Stryd and an oxygen uptake device (Cosmed K5). On a treadmill he measured the specific energy consumption (ECOR in kJ/kg/km) and the specific oxygen consumption (RE in ml O_2/kg/km) measured by the Cosmed. The shoes have also been tested on the road. He found on the treadmill that depending on the shoe, the oxygen consumption differed when running with the same wattage. Hechmann found that with the Nike Vaporfly (weight 200 grams) he was 8 to 10 seconds faster per kilometer than, for example, with the New Balance More (weight 300 grams). His stride length when using the Vaporfly turned out to be larger than normal.

In the following enumeration and figure, Hechmann summarized his research results for the gains of the various shoes he tested (size US 9½).
• 0 % Saucony Munchen (270 gram) en New Balance 1080 (280 gram)
• 1% New Balance More (300 gram)
• 2% New Balance Rebel, (200 gram), New Balance 1400 (200 gram) en
  Altra Duo (240 gram)
• 3% Newton distance (240 grams) and Adidas Adizero Takum Zen (180 grams)
• 4% Nike Vaporfly (200 gram)
• 6% Nike Vaporfly Next % (200 gram)

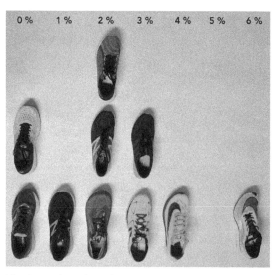

[6]Test af løbesko med Stryd wattmåler og Cosmed K5 Mobile testudstyr, C. Hechmann, https://www.hechmannsport.dk/post/test-af-l%C3%B8besko

5.   *Joubert and Jones*[7]

At Austin State University (Texas, USA), research was done on 7 models with a carbon plate. The 7 shoes studied in Texas are the Hoka RocketX, the Saucony Endorphin Pro, the Nike Alphafly, the Asics Metaspeed Sky, the Nike Vaporfly2, the New Balance RC Elite, the Brooks Hyperion Elite2, and a traditional shoe, the Asics Hyperspeed.

The shoes were tested by 12 runners of similar level. They did the 5 km in about 16 minutes. In random order, they each ran with the shoes twice. This included determining the running efficiency (Running Economy, RE) each time.

The study concludes that only the Asics Metaspeed and Nike Alphafly offer similar running economy improvements (4%) to the Nike Vaporfly2. Athletes who choose one of the other shoes studied are at a competitive disadvantage.

The Hoka RocketX and Brooks Hyperion Elite2 did not differ from the traditional Asics Hyperspeed. The other shoes performed 1 to 2% less than both Nike's and Asics Metaspeed and thus better than the Asics Hyperspeed, and mentioned Hoka and Brooks.

Conclusions and follow-up:

The carbon shoes undeniably have a great positive effect on energy consumption.

1. Nike Vaporfly's ECOR is 4% lower than the standard value of 0.98 kJ/kg/km.
2. The time savings of carbon shoes have now also been proven in various studies (and practice). Due to the impact of air-resistance, the time savings are just under 4% (for elite athletes 3.4%).
3. The effects are not the same for everyone and depend, among other things, on running style. With a limited flight phase, a responsive shoe is of less use.
4. The effects depend on the type and manufacture of the shoe. It can be expected that all manufacturers will become/remain active in this technological arms race. This means that the energy consumption and time savings of each shoe type will have to be determined separately (compared to the traditional shoes or compared to the new Vaporfly standard).

[7] A Comparison of Running Economy Across Seven Carbon-Plated Racing Shoes, D.P. Joubert and G.P. Jones, https://scholarworks.sfasu.edu/kinesiology/33/

PRACTICAL TIPS AND CASES

Applications in practice

5.1 10 Years of running research

Their professional careers made that running became less and less performance-oriented for Hans van Dijk and Ron van Megen. Until 2011. In that year Hans retired as emeritus-professor of water supply. Hans found an ally in lifelong running mate, colleague and friend Ron van Megen. Since then they published an article on running every week. With explanations about all aspects that affect your running performance or with analyses of actual sports performances.

Hans and Ron live in The Netherlands and are civil engineers. Their scientific approach is based on the laws of physics and physiology. Most of their articles has been published on ProRun.nl. You can also find them regularly in other Dutch and international running magazines and running websites. Meanwhile, they have published several books and over 500 articles.

Ron van Megen and Hans van Dijk

How did it start?

Hans started running in 1980. On the 4th of August, the day after Dutch athlete Gerard Nijboer won the silver medal in the marathon of the Olympic Games in Moscow. In his teens Hans had played soccer in Feyenoord Rotterdam FC, but not earlier then this date in 1980 Hans appeared to have also talent for running. Ron was infected by the running virus a few years earlier.

Together they became colleagues, they are friends and above all lifelong runners. With Sunday morning as a fixed moment for their long run together. They discuss the week and make new plans during these runs. Over the years they have trained more than 40,000 km together and have run races and workouts in beautiful places all over the world.

A busy job and family life meant that over the years the emphasis got less on performance and more and more on recreational running. When he retired early as professor at Delft University of Technology, Hans was given a Garmin watch with a heart rate chest strap by his students. Hans had not used anything like that before as he ran by feel. Ron already had a running watch, but used it only to see his completed training rounds afterwards. His heart rate chest strap remained unused.

In the joint long Sunday runs through nature, Hans's new watch quickly became the topic of conversation. They recognized numerical relationships between pace and heart rate. Engineers love numbers so they delved into the theory. With themselves as a test object, they were able to confirm not only the well-known relationship between pace and heart rate but many other relationships.

Because of the busy social life, they had gained some body weight. This quickly led to the confirmation that losing 1% of weight leads to a 1% faster running pace. If you go on a diet and lose 15%, like Hans did in 2012, you run 15% faster. The profit of more targeted training can be added to that.

This focus on the impact of relevant aspects in running made Ron running the same times again as he did in the early 1990s. Hans competed in his age group both on the road and on track for the Dutch national titles. The fun and passion also led to achievements at international tournaments.

Hans in the silver 5000 meter final M55 between the Russian combine of Alexandre Kaplenko (207) and winner Leonid Tikhonov (1120) during the World Masters Games in Turin (2013)

The Secret of Running

A lot of running literature was reviewed and tried out in practice. They also analyzed the performance of top athletes and recorded and documented everything. The basis of the book The Secret of Running was laid.

The first Dutch edition was published on 13 October 2013 and proved to be a bestseller. That was certainly also the case for the calculator on the website www.theSecretofRunning.com. Hundreds of runners each day visit this website to calculate the impact of the conditions on their running performance, or to have the time calculated at a different distance, in case of wind, height differences, altitude, running surface, low or high air pressure, the impact of aging and much more.

The Secret of Cycling

The easy to read accessibility of the book The Secret of Running with many short chapters in which always one aspect is explored led to the question to write the book The Secret of Cycling.
Hans and Ron are cycling enthusiasts, but were not practicing and did not

have a network in this branch of sports. Sports doctor and cycling coach Guido Vroemen was able to fill that gap sublimely with his broad experience and expertise. In June 2015, The Secret of Cycling rolled off the presses.

Cycling and running have many similarities as endurance sports. The use of power meters is very common among performance-oriented cyclists of any level. Power (wattage) is no more or less than the amount of energy you consume per second (kiloJoules (kJ) or kilocalories (kcal) per second).
With the laws of physics you can calculate the rolling resistance (tires, road surface), air resistance (wind), climbing resistance (slopes) and mechanical resistance (chain, gears). This resulted in the cycling model.
On www.theSecretofCycling.com, everyone can calculate the impact of all kinds of aspects on cycling performance.

The eye opener was that basically this cycling model is also suitable for running and other endurance sports like speed skating. These sports all are related to the same laws of physics and physiology. Speed skating is of course about sliding resistance instead of rolling resistance. When running there are no losses due to chain and gears. The universal calculation model for endurance sports was born.

THE UNIVERSAL THEORY OF SPORTS

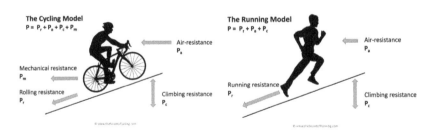

The Universal Theory of Sports. Basically, cycling and running are related to the same laws of physics.

Running power

With the insights gained into the concept of wattage (power) for cycling, it naturally came to mind how beautiful it would be if you could also work with power when running. Hans dived in the theory and perfected the running model with power.

Never before has running performance been so perfectly calculated, evaluated and performance predicted. All this was elaborated in the international editions of the book The Secret of Running.

There was only one problem. At that time running power meters did not exist. You could calculate wattages but unlike cycling you could not measure it while running. Early 2016 the first running power meters popped up. Stryd was a pioneer. Soon followed by Polar, Garmin, COROS, dedicated apps for smart phones, and more.

The Stryd running power meter attaches to the laces on your shoe and connects to your Garmin, Polar, COROS, Apple Watch or many other sports watches

Initially, like other power meters Stryd measured only the running resistance and climbing resistance. With an ingenious system, it later also measured the air-resistance. Stryd uses a measurement principle similar to the pitot tube known from flow theory. Stryd calls it a "wind port". Hans and Ron know pitot tubes from their water background. In the aircraft industry, this measurement method is commonplace for measuring flight speeds. Hans and Ron were a bit skeptical at first. Stryd then gave Hans and Ron the opportunity to test it themselves in the facilities of the German-Dutch Wind Tunnels (DNW). And there they became impressed and convinced.

Today more and more people in the athletics world take running power seriously. It is determined differently from the direct measurement of power from the force on the pedals of a bicycle. Some still don't consider the algorithm-calculated power as a real wattage. This category of people will also have problems with the speedometer in their car's dashboard. This speed has not been determined mechanically in years.

Hans checks Stryd's test setup in DNW's wind tunnel. On the treadmill Ray Maker (DC Rainmaker)

Weekly

In the meantime, the weekly publication of articles continued. For example, Hans and Ron have shown under which (unregulated) conditions a marathon under two hours is possible. Of course, they analyzed Eliud Kipchoge's attempt in Monza (Italy) and his success at the INEOS 1:59 Challenge in Vienna (Austria). With a tail wind on a long straight dike it would also have been possible.

Of course, they also studied Nike's new super shoes with carbon plates that are good for a better running performance. In the late 1990s something similar happened in speed skating when the clap skate was recognized by the ISU, widely introduced and speed skate became 3-5% faster just because of tech-development.

Hans and Ron also explained how great the leading group in the Standard Chartered Dubai Marathon 2020 worked together to the end, keeping each other out of the wind and ended up with 11 runners under 2:07. Between numbers 1 and 11 there were only 19 seconds. Of the 20 first finishers, 14 ran a PB.

How about the Andalusia marathon, on paper the fastest marathon in the world with an altitude difference of 1938 meters down and finish in Malaga (Spain). Downhill only! That was fast but also accompanied by injuries. The speed gain from the continuous decline of the course resulted in stress on muscles, tendons and knees.

Everyone knows that running performance decreases with the years. It's nice to know how much that is and how fast you would have run at 28 years with your current form. It motivates masters to continue.

Hans and Ron also evaluated the performance of elite cyclist Tom Dumoulin in the Tour de France. What difference does a kilo of body weight make? And many articles came along about the impact of temperature on running performance, sweat production and the limits of human performance.

International

The success of Hans and Ron's books and articles did not go unnoticed. Several book titles are available worldwide in English, German, Polish, Spanish or Italian. This is also reflected in a visit to the bilingual website www.theSecretofRunning.com. On this website you find a nice overview of all editions and appearances of the books.

Passion and pleasure in running are at the heart of this book. Koen de Jong, Ron van Megen and Hans van Dijk explain how to achieve better performances.

5.2 You bought a running power meter. What now?

Polar, Garmin, COROS, Power2Run and others offer running power. The information on how to get started with running power can be hard to find. COROS offers more information. Stryd provides a wealth of information on their website. Search engines are a great tool to find answers to any question you have. In this chapter we give you an introduction by taking Stryd as an example.

Attaching a Stryd to your shoelaces or setting up your watch is a breeze. But then what? This is a frequently asked question.

The first use

Unlike cycling power meters, running power meters need to know your height. Both need your weight. You therefore need to make sure you go into the settings of your watch or power meter to make sure the weight and height are correctly set.

Additionally, you need to configure your watch to show power data. Depending on the watch, you may need to add an app (for Garmin) or select the native power data fields like with COROS and Polar watches. If you use a foot pod like Stryd, you may need to pair it with your watch as well.

When you go for your first run, power is just a number on your watch. You can either learn about power by yourself, but is better to determine your power threshold (i.e., Functional Threshold Power (FTP) or Critical Power (CP)). Once you know your threshold power, you can easily use power zones or a power-based training plan.

There are several ways to determine your threshold power. You can use advanced software like Golden Cheetah or WK05 to analyze your own run data and determine your FTP. Polar has a test you can perform any time at your convenience. Stryd keeps track of all your runs, and based on your running data, it automatically calculates your threshold power (critical power). Lastly, you can go to a test center and have a professional help you determine your VO_2 max and FTP on a treadmill.

If you have a recent 5K or 10K time, you can use online calculators or the Stryd mobile app to determine your FTP or CP as well.

Daily Use

You can use power in many ways.

Just run. You can continue to run as you always do and learn yourself what power target works for you during all your workouts. You can use power to keep your effort the same regardless of terrain and wind. You are unlikely to get the most out of your power meter, though.

Use Power Zones. Most watches support power zones. Power zones work similar as heart rate zones. You will have easy, intermediate, and hard zones. For example, if you use Stryd zones, you can simply stay in zone 1 for easy run, zone 3 for tempo runs and zone 4 for 800-meter intervals.

Power-based Training Plans. The best method to use power meters is to switch to a power-based training plan. You can convert an existing heart rate or pace-based plan. You can also purchase a power-based plan from a coach in TrainingPeaks or Final-Surge. And COROS and Stryd offer free power-based plans in their ecosystems for various distances. In TrainingPeaks plans are offered by recognized coaches.

If you sign up for a power-based plan, you will get a calendar populated with your workouts. You are not locked in, you can typically change the day of your workout, delete if you need a break, or adjust the intensity. Typically, your workout can be loaded onto your watch (Garmin, COROS, Wahoo) and your watch will guide you through your workout as if a coach is biking next to you. When you execute a workout on your watch, each segment will end with a count-down to the next segment with audio and vibration cues. Typically, you can see the power target and duration of the upcoming segment.

This is a fun and easy way to train with power: stay in the "green" and avoid going too slow or too fast. This way you train by color, and you only need to pay attention to one thing while running.

What is great about power-based training is that plans are typically setup as a percentage of your FTP or CP. If your fitness improves, your threshold power also increases. Stryd users enjoy automatic adjustment of CP, but you can also do a test or use advanced software to calculate a new FTP. When your fitness changes, your plan automatically adjusts. This means that throughout a training cycle you will likely need to run faster to remain in the correct zone (your intensity and load will remain the same as you are in better shape).

You do not need to use any specific ecosystem. Typically, you can link your watch platform to any other service you like such as Strava, TrainingPeaks, etcetera. Software can keep track of your data, and it can be fun to see how your training compares to previous workouts.

Some software can build a power duration curve based on your training data. It will record your hardest effort for any duration (typically between 0 and 90 minutes). Software can then use that data to build a model for you that you can use to set a power target for any duration. For example, if you did a time trial of 10 and 20 minutes, the power duration curve can tell you your power target for 30 minutes. And you can easily find your FTP: simply select 60 minutes and see what is the power you can maintain.

The power duration curve can be a fun way to challenge yourself. Plan a workout by picking any duration and look for your modeled ability. Then you can create a workout where you aim to run at your modeled power target for the specified time. If you are in excellent shape, you can push yourself and try to beat the target. When you do this, your critical power likely will go up as well as you have gained fitness.

POWER DURATION CURVE

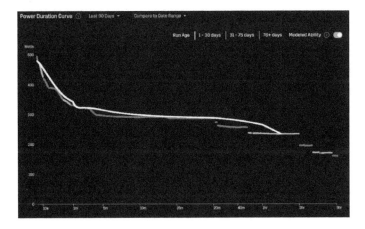

Running with power during an event

When you know your FTP or CP, you can optimize race performance by running with power. There are various ways to get a power target.

Using the Riegel equation. You can estimate a power target by deriving a power target based on FTP. Any online race calculator where you enter your race time for one distance to get a time or power estimate for another distance uses this equation. You can read more about this in the chapter The power-time relationship.

Using your Power Duration Curve. You can use the power duration curve to pick an estimated duration of your race and find the power that you can hold for that duration. The obvious disadvantage is that you need to know what time it will take you to run the race distance.

Using the Stryd Race Power Calculator. Stryd users have the advantage to have access to an advanced race power calculator. In the race power calculator, you can indicate which distance you are going to run. The calculator will give a prognosis of your race time and advice on the power to maintain in the race. This is based on your critical power (CP), your power duration curve, and your own running data. The Stryd systems keeps track of how your pace and power relate to each other, for a variety of inclines. The race calculator tracks under what conditions you trained, and you can adjust elevation, temperature, and humidity to know what your maximum performance will be during your race. For example, if you trained at elevation or hot temperatures, you could run much faster at sea level and optimal temperatures.

You can even load a FIT or GPX file with the details of the race course. This is helpful because hills will affect your race time (even if your power target does not). Some race organizations make them available on the website. And if you've run the race before, you can use last time's file.

In the example below Ron has put the Seven Hills Run in the race calculator. That 1:20:04 would not produce a personal best, but Ron was also not in great shape in the period in advance of this race.

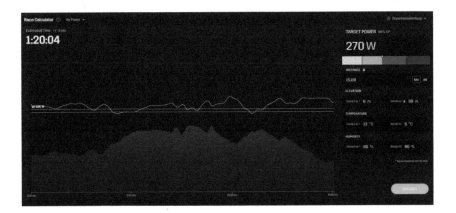

The graph shows that Ron can run it with 270 Watts (and then reach 1:20:04). The blue line shows that at a constant power (270 Watts) the uphill pace is slower and downhill faster to reach the fastest race time.

In addition to being able to enter races yourself in the race calculator, a few major marathons, such as Berlin are already pre-programmed. Nice to see what you could run there with your current shape.

Whatever method you use to calculate your race power target, when you are at the start of a race, you are not guessing what your pace should be for that day. You have a simple goal: stay as close to your power target as you can. When you keep effort the same, you will optimize your race. During a marathon that means that the first half will feel very easy as the power meter will moderate your pace. And at the end, you feel that your power meter is pushing you. When you finish, you will have spent all your energy and know that you ran the best race possible that day.

5.3 Tips for using Stryd training plans

In the previous chapter we explained to brand new owners how to use their running power meter. Stryd offer a variety of power-based training plans. Plans that change automatically if your fitness improves through training because they are linked to your personal critical power.

You can load these workouts into your Garmin watch with the help of the Stryd Workout IQ app. We explain how that works in this chapter. The Stryd training plans also fully integrate with Apple watch.
COROS watches are specially developed for use with Stryd, including the training plans. If you have a Polar or a Suunto, you will get the data of the Stryd on your data screen while running, but you need to remember what the program was for your workout. In practice, of course, that also works.

By the way, you are not stuck with the membership of Stryd to train with power workouts. You can convert workouts to power yourself and there are various platforms – such as TrainingPeaks and Final Surge – that are Stryd compatible. Those platforms typically allow you to purchase a training plan from renowned coaches. The "data-only" account with frequently used features of Stryd is sufficient, you do not need to sign up for the paid Stryd Membership.

At the end of this chapter, we give the tip to use your Stryd for speed and distance. That's typically much more accurate than the GPS on your watch. Remember to turn off automatic calibration on your watch. Otherwise, your watch will calibrate the Stryd to the GPS data which can lead to unexpected and undesired results.

Stryd Workout IQ app for Garmin
The advantage of the Stryd Workout App is that you automatically load ad-

vanced workout sessions into your watch. Beeps and vibrations alert you to the transition to the next block of the workout. It is not complicated to use. In this chapter we show you how things work using some images. This IQ app has to be installed in your Garmin watch in the usual way.

Workout

Stryd offers a range of workouts plans, for different distances and the number of days you can train per week. That's what we described in the previous chapter. You can choose a training plan from the Stryd app on your smart phone.

You start by tapping 'Stryd workout Plans' on the opening screen (Summary) of the Stryd app on your smart phone. Then you are asked what you want to train for. You can choose from Intro, 5K, 10K, half marathon or marathon.

If you do not know your Critical Power yet, we recommend you sign up for the Intro plan. This is a 2-week plan that has many easy runs (that can be skipped if you prefer) and a few workouts where you run as fast as you can for a short interval of varying durations. When you have completed this plan, Stryd will calculate your Critical Power which is the foundation for subsequent training plan (and training zones if you prefer to train by zone).

In this example, we assume you already have an accurate Critical Power number and choose the half marathon. The next question is when's that race? The question after that is also not illogical: when do you want to start training for that half?

TRAINING WITH POWER (1)

The screens also follow logically with questions about how many days you want to train in the week and how many hours per week that may be? Not to mention the question on which day you usually have time for a long workout?

If all that is answered, 2 workout plans have been proposed in this case. One with a limited size (Low Volume) of 4 days a week with an average of 4 hours of workouts per week and a more intensive (High Volume) for 6 days with an average of 7 hours per week.

Once the choice is made, the Stryd calendar fills up with workouts until race day.

TRAINING WITH POWER (2)

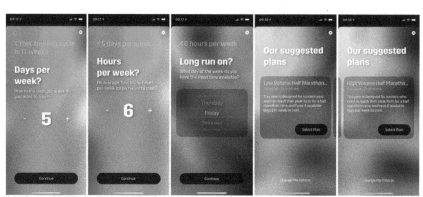

Where can you find the Stryd Workout App on your Garmin?

After you install the Stryd Workout app from the Garmin Connect IQ store, you can get the Stryd Workout App by pressing the button at the top right of your Garmin. You will then see the well-known menu in which you normally choose 'Running'. For the Stryd Workout App, scroll further down until you see 'Stryd Workout App' appear in the dark background area. Click. And you will be in the Stryd Workout App.

In the Stryd Workout App you can adjust the data screens, via 'Settings' and 'Data fields'. If you choose '3s Power' or '10s Power', the number value on your screen is a little less variable which make it easier to use for some runners. You also must program the username on your watch. The username allows you to fetch your workouts. If you are not sure about your Stryd user-

name, you can log in to Stryd PowerCenter and you can find your username on your profile page (top left corner of your screen).

The first workout

Make sure your Garmin is ready with your phone with the Stryd app. In the Stryd Workout App on your Garmin, you can get the workouts by first using the button at the top right of your Garmin to click on the 'Workouts' screen and then 'Fetch Workouts'. The workout sessions for the next days will appear in your Garmin (only workouts in the upcoming 5 days will be loaded).

Then, go to the 'x Workouts' field on your Garmin. Here you can see the x workouts received neatly by day and date. If the workout for Tuesday, for example, does not suit you, you can choose that workout on another day. Just like in the paid version of TrainingPeaks, you can swipe the workout from one day to the next if this suits you better (in the Stryd app or PowerCenter).

As a first try, Ron chose the 'Easy Run /w Strides' on Thursday. On your watch you can see how this workout is structured. You can view this in more detail in the Stryd app on your phone. This first workout consists of 2 blocks of 22 minutes in zone 1 'Easy'. In between there are 4 intervals in zone 4 of 30 seconds after which 60 seconds rest low in zone 1.

TRAINING WITH POWER (4)

The zone distribution is personal and linked to your Critical Power. Ron's CP currently stands at 294 Watts. If CP improves (or deteriorates) during the training cycle, the system adjusts the wattages with which you must run. This way you always train at the correct intensity for you.

On the road

As you already know, you get the best result in a race or time trial by keeping the wattage constant. You do this by varying the pace or running speed when conditions change. This is illustrated in the figure below. Uphill you run slower than average and downhill faster. Similarly with head and tail wind.

The Stryd Workout App screens on your Garmin help you maintain the right power and pace. The top field of the opening screen shows the current power. The color is green if you run within the range of the target power for the workout block in question. If you go too fast, the color of this field becomes red. Blue is too slow.

At the top of the Garmin screen, a countdown is displayed in 2 ways. A clock goes back to zero. And the green bar becomes shorter and shorter to the right until the block within the workout is done. At the beginning and at the end of such a block, screen-filling digits count down from 5 to 0. Beeps and vibrations support this. Not to be missed. You can hardly do the workout wrong.

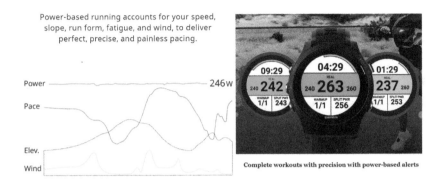

Power-based running accounts for your speed, slope, run form, fatigue, and wind, to deliver perfect, precise, and painless pacing.

Complete workouts with precision with power-based alerts

At home you can evaluate your achievements. The results are available in Garmin Connect, in PowerCenter and, if you use it, also in TrainingPeaks or similar other tools.

TRAINING WITH POWER (5)

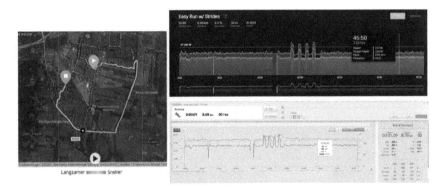

Speed and distance

You can set up your Garmin watch to use either Stryd for pace and/or distance or GPS. It is a good choice to use the foot pod. The Stryd is much more accurate than GPS. You'll notice that on the track where GPS has difficulty with the turns. You will experience it when you run beneath wet, thick foliage of trees that interfere with GPS reception. And you will notice it in the city if you run along tall buildings. For Stryd, it doesn't matter if you run indoors or outdoors as it does not need GPS to be accurate. Ron's Stryd indicated exactly the 200 meters of an indoor track. The smart instruments in the Stryd –inertial measurement units (IMU's) – measure your movements exactly.

To set the Stryd on your Garmin for speed and distance, go into you're the watch's menu. You click through to 'Sensors and accessories'. You look up 'Foot Sensor' and see if you already paired your watch. If not, have the watch look for new foot pod sensors while you move your Stryd. Stryd will advertise itself as FP-xxxxx (ignore FP-STRYD if shown on the watch). Once you have paired your Stryd with your Garmin watch, you can set both 'Distance' and 'Speed' to 'Always'. In the same menu you see 'Cal. Factor'. In principle, it should be at 100 (unless you have done a test on a measured track, refer to the Stryd knowledge base for details). In the same menu, you have to disable 'Automatic calibration'. This is typically recommended as autocalibration with GPS can lead to unexpected results!

Stryd does not need to be calibrated for most runners. You don't have to do anything before you start, but if in doubt, you can always test it on a track where you know that the distance is correct. For example, you can run on a certified athletic track. If you run 0.30 m from the inner edge of lane 1 of a 400-meter track (with the Stryd on the laces of your left shoe), you will cover exactly 400 m in one lap. You need to run several laps for good results, we recommend 8 laps with your typical running shoes at regular pace (85% of CP). Stryd has a detailed protocol that is slightly different and help you calibrate your Stryd. You can find details on stryd.com/support.

In the exceptional case that the distance according to Stryd deviates from the actual distance, you can adjust the calibration factor. Divide actual distance with Stryd recorded distance and multiply with 100. Then you can enter the calibration factor in the Sensor and Accessory menu of your Garmin watch.

5.4 Laboratory testing

Performance labs of sports medical centers offer a variety of tests. In this chapter we elaborate on the testing of the aerobic system of a runner on a treadmill and provide context with running power and energy cost of running. In doing so, we extend the conceptual framework of the more traditional parameters with running power for you.

To test the aerobic system the load is increased step-by-step by increasing the speed of the treadmill. Such a test goes beyond your aerobic and anaerobic thresholds until you (nearly) reach your maximum effort level. This is called the threshold test. This test provides an accurate assessment of your threshold speed, threshold heart rate and even threshold power.

Threshold Test

This test is used to determine the threshold accurately. In addition to heart rate (HR) and blood pressure, the composition of the exhaled air is measured breath-by-breath, including the concentrations of oxygen (O_2) and carbon dioxide (CO_2). The software generates various graphs that show how energy production in the body changes. During the test, various parameters are determined which provide information about your physical fitness. With this information, individual limitations can be diagnosed. Also training plans and training advice can be optimized.

Protocol Threshold Test

To ensure that the body gets the opportunity to reach a new equilibrium at the next step, the duration of a step should be sufficiently long. A 3-minute step length is suitable, shorter steps are not advised. The starting speed is determined based on previous performances of the runner. It should be at least a few km/h slower than the 10K race speed. Each step the speed is increased by 1 km/h. Once the anaerobic threshold has been reached, the duration of the steps is reduced to one minute until the maximum speed is reached.

Which parameters are measured?

Ventilation:

Ventilation is the volume of exhaled air (VE) in 1 minute. The VE is calculated from the number of breaths per minute, the respiratory rate or frequency (Rf), and the volume per breath, the Tidal Volume (TV).

$$VE = Rf*TV$$

At rest the Rf is about 10 - 12 times per minute and the TV is about 500 - 1000 ml. Thus, the VE at rest is about 5 to 10 l/min. During maximal effort the respiratory rate Rf may increase to 60 - 70 l/min and the TV up to 3000 - 4000 ml (depending on total lung volume). So during maximum effort the VE can be up to 200 l/min or more.

Circulation

The circulation, also known as cardiac output (CO) is calculated from the heart rate (HR) and the volume of blood circulated per stroke (SV).

$$CO = HR*SV$$

At rest, the resting heart rate (RHR) is about 50 - 60 bpm (well-trained athletes have lower values) and the SV is about 60 - 80 ml. So the CO at rest is some 4 to 5 l/min.

During maximum effort HR may increase up to 200 bpm (depending on age) and the SV of well-trained athletes to 150 - 200 ml. Consequently, the CO during maximum effort can increase to 30 - 40 l/min.

The stroke volume SV cannot yet be measured simply during a test. The heart rate HR is determined from the electrocardiogram (ECG).

Oxygen concentration:
During the test the oxygen content in every breath is determined. By determining the difference with the outside air (20.93% oxygen), the oxygen uptake by the body can be calculated. At maximum effort the maximum oxygen uptake (VO_2 max) can be determined.

Carbon dioxide concentration:
The amount of carbon dioxide is determined in the exhaled air and compared with the outside air (0.03% CO_2). Consequently, the CO_2 production by the body can be calculated.

Respiratory Quotient (RQ) or Respiratory Exchange Ratio (RER):
This parameter indicates the sources of energy that your body uses. The RQ is the amount of CO_2 produced (in l/min) divided by the amount of O_2 used (in l/min).

$RQ = VCO_2/VO_2$
If only fatty acids are used RQ is 0.7. If glycogen (carbohydrates) are burned exclusively RQ is 1.0. At an RQ of 0.85, the fuel mix consists of 50% fatty acids and 50% glycogen. This parameter is useful to assess the fat and glycogen consumption during various efforts.

Equivalents (VE/VO_2 and VE/VCO_2)
These parameters say something about the amount of air required to ventilate 1 liter of oxygen, or exhale 1 liter of carbon dioxide.

Aerobic threshold (first ventilatory threshold):
This is the threshold where the production of lactic acid starts. At this point the lactic acid can still be easily removed and broken down by your body. Consequently, the concentration of lactic acid hardly increases. This threshold is between Zone 1 and Zone 2. Graphically this point can be recognized as the point where the VE/VO_2 starts rising.

Anaerobic threshold (second ventilatory threshold):
From this point on you produce so much lactic acid that it cannot be broken down sufficiently. So lactic acid starts to accumulate. The further you get above

this threshold, the shorter you can maintain this intensity. This threshold is between Zone 3 and Zone 4. Graphically this point can be recognized as the point where both VE/VO$_2$ and VE/VCO$_2$ no longer remain constant and will rise.

The maximum oxygen uptake capacity (VO$_2$ max):
The maximum oxygen uptake is measured in milliliters per minute (ml/min). In order to make the parameter comparable with other runners (and changes in your weight) it is divided by the body weight (in kg) and expressed as ml/kg/min.

The running economy (RE):
This is the amount of oxygen that is used by the runner to run 1 km at a certain submaximal speed. At every (submaximal) speed the oxygen uptake is measured in ml/min/kg and the running economy can be calculated in ml/kg/km. As an example we use an oxygen uptake at 12 km/h of 45 ml/min/kg. Consequently, this runner has an RE 5 x 45 = 225 ml/kg/km , as it takes him 5 minutes to run 1 km.

Running economy is a very important parameter because it tells you how efficient your running style is, how much energy you use to run 1 km. World class marathon runners can have an RE of 180 ml O$_2$/kg/km. Average runners have an RE of 210 - 240 ml O$_2$/kg/km.

Energy cost of running (ECOR)
In an earlier chapter we looked at the impact of the energy cost of running ECOR (in kJ/kg/km). We can also express the energy cost of running in terms of the specific oxygen uptake (in ml O$_2$/kg/km).

This can be determined in the laboratory with a treadmill test as explained above. As the energy value of 1 ml of O$_2$ is equal to 19.5 J and the metabolic efficiency can be set at 25% (for elite athletes; for fitness runners about 23%), the following relationship holds:

ECOR = (19.5*0.25/1000)*RE

This means an RE of 201 ml O$_2$/kg/km is equivalent to our standard value for ECOR of 0.98 kJ/kg/km. Obviously, the ECOR and the RE are not the same for all runners and in all conditions.

For a true calculation this test has to be done with force plates. Bearing in mind that a running power meter does not measure forces but accelerations and uses an algorithm to calculate power, the specific energy cost of running ECOR can be approached at the treadmill test by wearing a running power meter only. However, this ECOR value is great for evaluation of performances as it takes the impact of speed, hills and wind (only Stryd is precise at the date of writing this book) into account.

The ECOR-value (in kJ/kg/km) can be easily calculated (even after every workout) by dividing the average specific power (Watts/kg) by the average speed (in m/s).

Relationship FTP - VO$_2$ max

In a treadmill test also the Functional Threshold Power (FTP) can be determined. Point of attention for as well VO$_2$ max and FTP is the incline of the treadmill. The incline has to compensate the lack of running wind on a treadmill. A functionality to note is the Stryd support for power changing when incline changes. When incline changes, Power changes accordingly. Also on a treadmill. In other words Stryd recognizes the treadmill incline. Aspects influencing VO$_2$ max determination apart from the incline this way are a.o. room temperature, absence of wind cooling.

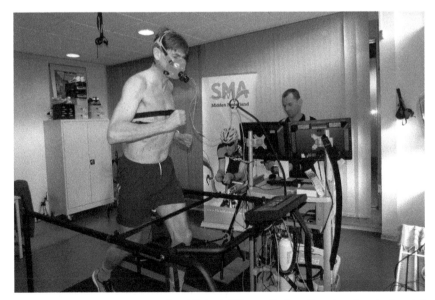

Ron at the treadmill for a combined ergo spirometry and running power test.

$$FTP = 0.072 * VO_2 \, max$$

Example: $VO_2 \, max = 51 \, ml/kg/min$. $FTP = 0.072 * 51 = 3.67 \, Watts/kg$

Training post laboratory test

Measuring VO_2 is an excellent way to determine your fitness. If you could always run with a VO_2 device, you could optimize your metabolic training. However, running with a VO_2 device is not practical or fun. You can use a power meter designed for runners instead as these tools mimic a VO_2 measurement device, are cheaper, and are not noticeable while running.

If you used a power meter during your laboratory test, you or your coach can adjust your training. For example, you will know exactly what your power number is at VO_2 max. This can help tune your intervals to just the right target power.

As your fitness will change over time, you will need to repeat the laboratory test regularly (every 4 to 6 weeks) if you want to keep training at the optimal level based on your VO_2 max. Of course, you can also rely on systems like automatic critical power (as calculated by the Stryd system or different software) instead as that is easier and cheaper.

5.5 Vary in your training

We were excited to meet a master athlete aging 80 years and full of ambitions. He shared some valuable learnings from his running career. He told he jogged the same course twice a week. Nothing wrong with that! Exercise is healthy. Running is fun. You are outdoors and you enjoy the surroundings. And after having a shower afterwards you feel good and you pop on the couch with a satisfied feeling or return full of energy to your desk for your daily work.

For many runners this is enough. But if you do what you always do, you get what you always got. You will not become a better, faster runner. With the same course at the same pace, boredom can also hit, and the pleasure of running could gradually disappear. Targeted varied training is the solution.

Exercise is healthy. Running is fun. You are outdoors and you enjoy the surroundings.

How do you vary your training?

The possibilities to bring variety to your training are manifold. For example, think of several different routes, longer and shorter, in the woods, on a mountainous trail, or along meadows. You will see different landscapes slowly changing with the seasons, no run is ever the same.

Whatever route you run, Strava segments are everywhere. On one of those Strava segments, you go all-out. In the Strava platform you can see afterward how your performance comparers to previous times you ran the segment.

You can join a running group or athletics club. Typically, you can run at your own level. One or two joint workouts a week are a motivator to head out. If the group has a coach, you do not need to worry about variation in your training. The coach will build variation into your training for you. And it is fun! You get to know new people who share your passion for running. If you want to do more workouts in a week, the trainer likely has tips or a training plan for you.

Training plans

The training plans of your running group or athletics association are likely well designed. Hans and Ron are members of the Amersfoort athletics club Altis. For each calendar day, 7 days a week, there is a workout scheduled. The pace of your training runs is linked your 10K race time. This way the training plan will have you run at your level.

Most runners cannot train 7 days a week, and this is not recommended for everyone in most cases. That is why the Altis' plan indicates which workouts you can drop if you can only run 6, 5, 4 or 3 times a week.

The program is not the same year-round. During the build-up period to a race, the plan reduces volume and intensity close to race day to be at your best at the start of your race. This is also applies during the recovery period. And when preparing for an event, you will stress your body more with harder and longer workouts. Periodizing throughout the year and training specifically for a particular race brings variety and helps you to become a better runner.

A plan helps many runners to put on their running shoes. Having a plan makes it easy to get out of bed when you "have to" do a certain workout that day. Of course, you are not obliged to do anything, but once you start a plan you will find the structure helps you.

The plan should suit you

Our master athlete followed our advice but got the feeling with a certain plan that sometimes he had to run the long runs so slowly that he almost fell over. At other training sessions he had to run so fast that he invariably got sore legs.

It is fine to go a bit faster during slow runs if it feels comfortable. Remember that running slow is important. Too fast, and the training will have little effect. And if the prescribed fast paces feel too hard, it is fine to slow down a bit. The difference between minimum and maximum heart rate might be smaller for some than for others. This is a point of discussion with your coach. This way you can tailor a plan to your needs.

Using another plan, our master athlete felt like he was running four races in a week. That worked out well for him because it felt fine with it, but of course this is not recommended in general. You risk getting injured. Easy recovery runs are necessary for everyone!

Plans are plentifully available

On the Internet you can find running plans in abundance, both paid and free. TrainingPeaks and FinalSurge are good places to find excellent paid training plans. Stryd users can sign up for training plans for distances from 5K to marathon free of charge.

Many coaches use TrainingPeaks or FinalSurge so that they can follow performance of their athletes remotely. And some coaches offer a service to customize a training plan for you. While these plans are not free but useful if you do not want to join a running group or athletics club.

With a Stryd foot pod, the coach is literally on your shoe. The data that Stryd running power meter generates during your workouts and races automatically adjust your plan as needed. If you get stronger or if your fitness diminishes, your power targets will change. We are convinced this approach is the future.

What elements should be in a plan?

Depending on what you want to achieve, plans differ. In the table below we have summarized the possible training goals of the elements in a training. In a good plan you will find a mix of all training types. In the table FTP stands for functional threshold power, the wattage you can sustain for one hour of running. HR max is your maximum heart rate. In the table we included heart rate so that you can relate heart-based training to power-based workouts.

Finally, a general observation is that most modern training plans prescribe a lot of running time in zone 1. The training elements in other zones are generally short with multiple repetitions with intermittent recovery in zone 0 or 1. The idea is to improve during short and hard training segments but take enough time to recover and avoid injury. If you always run in zone 3 or higher, you certainly will get injured.

Zone	Training goal	Training form	Power %FTP	TrainingPeaks-zones (%HRmax)
0	Circulation in muscles	Warming up and recovery training	60 - 70	n.a.
1	Improvement aerobic capacity and aerobic efficiency	Endurance training (10 - 30 km)	70 - 80	<85%
2	Improvement transition from aerobic to anaerobic system	Tempo endurance training with long tempo blocs (3 - 5 km)	80 - 90	85 - 89%
3	Improvement lactate threshold power and anaerobic efficiency	Extensive interval training with longer blocs (1000 m)	90 - 100	zone 3: 90 - 94% zone 4: 95 - 99%
4	Improvement lactate tolerance and VO$_2$ max	Intensive interval training with shorter blocs (400 m)	100 - 110	zone 5a: 100 - 102% zone 5b: 103 - 106%
5	Improvement anaerobic capacity	Speed training (200 m intervals)	110 - 130	zone 5c: > 106%
6	Improvement explosive power	Sprint training (50 - 100 m)	>130	n.a.

5.6 How to convert your workout description to running power?

Quite a few questions from our readers are about the use of a power meter for training plans that are not yet available for power. We can answer his question in general because a running power meter is independent of the training method. It's an instrument, not a method. Neither are a GPS running watch or a heart-rate chest strap.

You don't need more than wattage on your running watch.

Quick and easy

We give an example how you can easily calculate the wattage with which you have to run according to your workout: Suppose you have to run a block in 10K race pace. You weigh 70 kg and run the 10K in 50:00. The block actually requires a pace of 5:00/km. Over 1000 meters (1 km) this is 300 seconds (5:00), so 1000/300 = 3.33 meters/second.

The wattage (power) with which you have to run this particular block in your workout can be calculated as:

3.33 m/s*1.04*70 kg = 242 Watts.

Another block could be to run a 400 meters in 28 seconds per 100 meters. This requires a running speed of 100/28 = 3.57 m/s.
Your corresponding wattage is 3.57 m/s*1.04*70 kg = 260 Watts.

This way you can calculate the wattage for all situations. Whether you need to run an endurance run, blocks, or intervals over a certain distance or duration. You can remember the required wattages or you put the workout in your running watch.

What is that 1.04?

The 1.04 is the specific energy consumption. And stands for energy consumption (in kiloJoules) per kilogram of body weight per kilometer. The unit is kJ/kg/km. The widely used term is ECOR (Energy Cost of Running) for this specific energy consumption.

The default value you often see is 0.98 kJ/kg/km. The value 0.98 is for running resistance only. In the 1.04 we also included the resistance of the running wind as well as the average metabolic efficiency of runners at different levels. This is explained in detail in the chapter From Target Power to race time. Why factor 1.04?. The 0.98 kJ/kg/km can therefore be used on a treadmill and 1.04 outside at windless days.

Is it always 1.04?

Unfortunately, the value 1.04 kJ/kg/km does not apply to everyone. You shouldn't be surprised if, as a recreational runner, you have to use 1.07 or maybe 1.08 instead of 1.04 because of your running style or the level you qualify as runner.

How do you know your ECOR?

If you want to know your ECOR exactly, it's good to check out a few results from your races or workouts at race pace. Take days with little wind, flat and paved course, and distances of the order of 5 to 15K.

You calculate your ECOR from the average power and average pace at which you have run. When you take a few road races or fast endurance workouts, you have a good indication of your personal running efficiency (which you might be able to improve through training).

An example for a 70 kg runner: you have run on average 250 Watts at an average pace of 4:53/km, i.e. 1000 meters in 293 seconds = 3.41 m/s.

You calculate the ECOR by dividing the wattage by your weight (250/70 = 3.57 Watts/kg) and by the running speed (3.57 Watts/kg)/(3.41 m/s) = ECOR 1,047 kJ/kg/km. Rounded 1.05.

If you do this calculation for several situations, you have a good indication of the personal value you can use instead of 1.04 in future.

Remember that if there are many altitude differences in the course, or when there is a strong wind, the ECOR is always higher. After all, it will cost you more energy to run at the same pace under these conditions. The ECOR is lower if you run in a group all the time. That is one of the reasons that Eliud Kipchoge could run the sub2 hours marathon in Vienna. It is also the reason that you have to determine your personal ECOR with little wind on a flat and paved course.

Does it matter 1.04 or 1.07?

Yes and no. It means that with the same human power you can run a few percent faster. 3% difference for a marathon in 3:30 equates to about 6 minutes difference in race time. If you do 4 hours on the marathon the difference is about 7.5 minutes. So, it certainly matters when you are a performance-oriented runner. And no, when you run for fun and health only.

Your personal human engine has a certain power. From the calculations earlier in this chapter you can conclude that you can keep a higher pace when you run more efficiently (with lower ECOR).
Furthermore, you see that your weight is important. If you gained weight, the wattage drops per kg. At the same power, you'll run slower.

Remember, a running power meter does not measure forces. A running power meter measures accelerations and uses an algorithm to calculate power. Running power meter's ECOR presently do not include the impact of differences due to surface (e.g. track or beach) and shoes (e.g. training shoes or super shoes with a carbon plate).

The ECOR calculated this way comprises aspects as your cadence (typical for running power meters), and climb resistance (hills). With a Stryd power meter this ECOR also comprises air-resistance (Air Power).

5.7 Convert an existing training plan to a power plan

Training plans are widely available on the Internet. It starts with the athlete's goals: medium or long-distance? Or is it an athlete who runs a variety of races every year and wants to run a marathon? The number of days and the amount of time the athlete has available is another consideration. Can a runner train every day or is it necessary to schedule recovery days?

And of course, training is not just about following a plan. The evaluation and adjustments are equally important for an athlete working towards a great performance.

The training doctrine based on running with power is the same as common approaches. The human body is the same. Heart, lung, muscles, and your metabolism remain are not different. A conventional training plan can be easily converted to a power based plan. Once you start running with power, you gain experience and can fine-tune as needed.

Pace

We give an example of how to calculate the wattage the athlete has to run according to the workout of the training plan: Suppose the athlete has to run a segment at 10K race pace. Say, the athlete weighs 70 kg and runs the 10K in 50:00. The workout then actually requires a pace of 5:00/km. Over 1000 meters (1 km) this is 300 seconds (5:00), so 1000/300 = 3.33 meters/second.
The wattage (power) required to run that block is 3.33 m/s*1.04*70 kg = 242 Watts.

Another workout could be a 400-meter run in 28 seconds per 100 meters. In this case the running speed is 100/28 = 3.57 m/s. The corresponding wattage can be calculated as 3.57 m/s*1.04*70 kg = 260 Watts.

With this method, wattage can be calculated for all paces. Regardless of whether it is an endurance run, blocks, or interval over a certain distance or duration.

Like other training methods, a power-based training will be in a target range between 5 to 20 Watts as it is near impossible to run exactly at one exact power number.

If you want to know where that factor 1.04 comes from, we refer to the previous chapter.

If you want to avoid doing math, you can also run at the required speed and check the power values after your run (assuming you ran on flat terrain without much wind). You then get to know the power target for all paces used in your training plan and can easily convert to power which will then work in any condition.

Heart rate

For the conversion of a schedule based on heart rate to power, the table in the earlier chapter Vary in your training can be taken. Take the corresponding percentage of the FTP with heart rate for the training goal.

In this case, FTP of the athlete must be known. This Functional Threshold Power is the power that an athlete can sustain for an hour. If the athlete has done an hour-long race in the past few weeks, you will have an excellent baseline. Otherwise, a 10K time trial can work. The power value in the athlete's personal power duration curve (at 60 minutes) is another option to know the FTP. A specific test of shorter duration can also be a good alternative. See the chapter Determine your ftp and your training zones.

Critical Power (Stryd)

The Stryd system automatically calculates critical power (CP) value, which is defined as the threshold at which the dominant type of fatigue your body experiences changes. Often the time coincidences with the duration an athlete can run a 10K race. For performance-oriented runners, time would be (much) shorter than an hour. Consequently, CP can be a few percentage points higher (maximum 5%) than FTP.

Why 5%? This 5% applies to an athlete who runs 10K in 30 minutes. As a general rule of the thumb: doubling or halving the distance or time makes a difference of 5% in wattage. During a 5K the athlete can run with 5% more power than during the 10K. The half marathon runs the athlete with 5% lower power than a 10K for the best performance.

In the table below, we present (a part of) a training plan we borrowed from our athletics club Altis. We worked out a two-weeks sample plan.

The table applies to an athlete with a CP (critical power) of 302 Watts. He got this value from his Stryd. Stryd automatically adjusts the CP. When the athlete improves through training, the CP value increases and the athlete benefits from training at higher power. If the CP decreases, the athlete likely should slow down to avoid overreaching and start building fitness again.

In the second week of the schedule, a race is scheduled on Tuesday. For the 10K distance, the athlete should run at CP (300 Watts in this case). For a 5K, the power target should be 315 Watts (5% higher than 10K power).

Athlete data	CP 302 Watts (3.7 Watt/kg)						
Name	82 kg						
Monday week 1	Tuesday week 1	Wednesday week 1	Thursday week 1	Friday week 1	Saturday week 1	Sunday week 1	
10x200 m repeats with 200 m rest	core training sportschool	4x1000 m with 400 m rest	30 min easy	60 min 10x90 sec repeats with 150 sec rest	30 min easy with 10x20 sec strides with 40 sec rest	90 min fartlek	
zone 5 and zone 0		zone 3 and zone 0	zone 1	zone 2 andn zone 4	zone 1 and zone 5	zone 3	
110-130% and 60-70%		90-100% and 60-70%	70-80%	80-90% and 100-110%	70-80% and 110-130%	average 97%	
330-390 Watts and 180-210 Watts		270-300 Watts and 180-210 Watts	210-240 Watts	240-270 Watts and 300-330 Watts	210-240 Watts and 330-390 Watts	average 290 Watts	
Monday week 1	Tuesday week 1	Wednesday week 1	Thursday week 1	Friday week 1	Saturday week 1	Sunday week 1	
rest	race 5 K or 10 K	rest, optional easy 30 min	30 min easy with 5x60 sec repeats with 60 sec rest	90 min 3x10min repeats with 5 min rest	60 min easy with each 10 min 1 min acceleration	90 min fartlek	
	zone 4	zone 0	zone 1 and zone 4	zone 2 and zone 3	zone 1 and zone 4	zone 3	
	5 K in 105% or 10 K in 100%	60-70%	70-80% and 100-110%	80-90% and 90-100%	70-80% and 100-110 watt	average 97%	
	315 Watts or 300 Watts	180-210 Watts	210-240 Watts and 300-330 Watts	240-270 Watts and 270-300 Watts	210-240 Watts and 300-330 Watts	average 290 Watts	

5.8 Power-based interval training

Typically, you run many miles at a slow pace in training plans. The purpose of such workouts is to train you to run for a long period of time.

With intervals and running in blocks at a higher pace you accustom your body to a high speed. With clever combinations of speed, rest, and repetitions, your coach ensures that your running economy improves. For middle and long distance runners, the energy sources are mainly aerobic glycogen and fatty acid burning. In this chapter we do not have the intention to provide as a complete workout The power requirements for the intervals in this chapter are intended as building blocks for a workout.

Interval training makes you a better runner

Many serious runners train at least once a week with their athletics club on the track. On another day of the week, they train for themselves, or with a group, and do a bit longer intervals, speed work or hills according to the design of their training plan.

The added value is that you can train at higher intensity with intervals. It improves your speed, VO_2 max and anaerobic threshold. The objective may also be to train your energy systems (you have four!). Or to get your body used to lactic acid. This type of training is not as stressful as a race because in between the intervals you are allowed some recovery.

Depending on the objective, the coach varies the length of the intervals and the intermediate rest in the training plan. The coach also varies the pace during the intervals. Usually, coaches define a base intensity as 100%. In a rest week this can be reduced to 95% or even 90%. In the race period, the intensity can be 105%, or even 110%.

Typical the coach divides the group based on the 10K-times of the runners. You run in a group that is about as fast as you are. The number of seconds per 100 meters you have to run depends on your level, the interval distance and the intensity. This all seems to be the coach's secret. When you train with a power meter, it is no longer a secret to you.

Power-based interval training

In this chapter we explain how you can calculate the base-power of your intervals. First you need to know your Functional Threshold Power (FTP), which is the power (wattage) that you can sustain for 60 minutes. As earlier explained there are several ways to assess your personal FTP.

It can be even simpler done. You can have your FTP determined with the calculator on our website www.theSecretofRunning.com. You enter the distance and time of a fast race and find on the second to last tab your calculated FTP in Watts/kg. This number you need to multiply by your body weight. For Ron this is currently 3.25 Watts/kg at 80 kg, so 260 Watts.

In the table below you can see the percentage of your FTP that you should use as basic (!) Target Power for interval distances.

Interval distance [m]	Percentage FTP [%]
2000	100%
1600	102%
1200	104%
1000	107%
800	109%
600	114%
400	120%
200	126%
100	133%

The percentages increase for short interval distances because your anaerobic energy systems kick in to supply extra energy. However, your anaerobic fuel supply is limited. For this reason high powers and fast speeds can only maintained for short periods.

The graph below also gives these percentages. In the graph we have also drawn a line that indicates the maximum theoretical power supplied by the energy systems of the human engine. That is the limit of your human power. In an interval workout it is of course not intended to run that fast. It's no race. If you do, you will miss your training objective and may get injured.

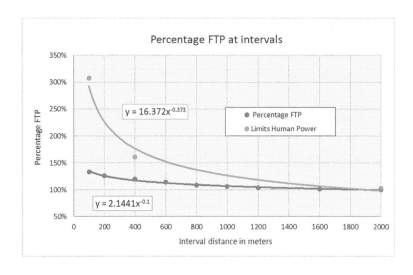

Practical examples Hans and Ron

As practical examples, we use the interval data of authors Hans and Ron. Hans runs 10K in 38 minutes. Ron currently needs about 51 minutes. Their coach traditionally specifies the required pace in terms of seconds per 100 meter for the various intervals. The table shows their corresponding power targets for the intervals. For the average runner this can be easily done with the formula:

P = 100/t*1.04*m

In the formula you enter for t the number of seconds per 100 meter and for m your body weight (in kg) to get the power P (in Watts). In the chapter From Target Power to race time. Why factor 1.04? you can read more about the factor 1.04.

Examples	Hans 58 kg		Ron 80 kg	
Interval distance [m]	pace (sec/100 m)	power (Watts)	pace (sec/100 m)	power (Watts)
1200	24.5	246	30.5	273
1000	24	251	30	277
800	23.5	257	29.5	282
600	23	262	29	287
400	22	274	28	297
200	20	302	26	320
100	18	335	24	347

The table clearly shows that Hans needs less power than Ron and still runs faster. Obviously, this is related to Hans' lower body weight.

5.9 Training threshold power

A power-based training plan improves your running performance. But not all workouts immediately increase your threshold power. Many professional coaches provide power-based training plans for runners. You can get these plans on paper, but often it is convenient to purchase plans in a platform like TrainingPeaks. In that case you do not need to memorize the workout while running as many sports watches will guide you through your training like a coach. You will have a trainer on your wrist! Runners that use Stryd can opt for free training plans available in the Stryd ecosystem.

One important point is that most training plans are based on a percentage of your threshold power or power zones which also depend on your threshold power. We can define threshold power in various ways. For example, you could use FTP which is the maximum power you could run for 60 minutes. Stryd uses Critical Power, which is defined as the threshold at which the dominant type of fatigue your body experiences changes (which often coincides with the power you can hold for a 10K race).

You therefore need to determine your personal threshold power. There are various methods. You can do a 5K or 10K race, a shorter test that consists of two shorter duration high intensity intervals. There is software available that can track your threshold power as well, such as Golden Cheetah and WK05. Stryd owners can use Stryd's automatic Critical Power which adjust your threshold power if needed and thus automatically adjusts your training zones and intensity (you will need to run faster to remain in the same zone).

While software can track your fitness, you will not see your threshold power increase after each run. Most software relies on actual training data, and only if you exceed a previous effort will your threshold power increase.

In this chapter we answer a frequently asked question about the Stryd training plans, Critical Power (CP) and power duration curve.

Philosophy

More experienced runners know that not all training plans are structured in the same way. That's not necessarily wrong. Not everyone is the same. And the insights into what a good training approach is are evolving. Older runners will tell you that they made a lot more kilometers or miles than is common today. And preferably they turned every workout into a race.

Many runners without a coach train at the wrong intensity. It is a simple mistake that silently hinders runners at all levels. It doesn't have to be this way. Most coaches prescribe a variety of intensities. With a proper training plan, many runners will run slower on easy days and long runs but will run at higher intensity during intervals and time trials.

Your own level

The number of training plans that exist is overwhelming. Most are for a specific distance, and you can often choose based on your own time availability and how many days you can run. Whether you're a seasoned athlete or a brand new one, the right training plan is an essential part of preparing for your next race.

The building blocks (workouts) of such a plan are linked to your personal threshold power in Watts. Threshold power says something about your condition. In that sense, it is like VO_2 max, the best-known and traditionally most used indicator for determining your fitness.

Well-designed plans automatically adapt when you improve fitness. To keep the same training effect, you will need to increase your running pace. Good plans will continue to increase stress during a training cycle so that you become fitter and better prepared for your event.

Building blocks

If you have chosen a certain training plan, you can indicate when the race is (typical training cycles are between 12 and 20 weeks). You also indicate on which day you usually have time for a long run. You can see your upcoming workout in a platform like TrainingPeaks or the Stryd ecosystem.

Training plans can be modified if needed. For example, if you can't train one day, you can easily move that workout to another day. If you are not feeling well it is often better to modify your training week rather than force yourself to complete a challenging training.

As indicated above, long workouts are a lot slower than many runners are used to. Now and then there is a time trial in the plan, where you go all out for a longer period of time. Most workouts consist of strides, intervals and blocks in which you have to go full out for the "prescribed" wattages. These are the workouts to improve your base speed. That is not the purpose of the long training sessions. If you did, you would have to recover longer and on balance you would benefit less from your workout.

Time versus distance based training plans

You can select a training plan based on distance or time. While distance is often convenient for planning purposes, time is better for slower runners to manage stress on the body. A 20K run is not the same for an elite runner as it is for a beginner, but a one hour run at the same percentage of threshold power is equivalent! Distance is not a goal in itself. The amount of stress on the body should be build and managed carefully is important. Stress is measured by comparing each second of the workout with threshold power. A long slow run can have the same stress as a short high intensity workout.

During a training cycle, each training has a specific purpose. Often an explanation is provided. We give three examples of a training from a Stryd training plan.

EXAMPLE 1: **FARTLEK**

Your workout today calls for four repeats of 5:00 at 95-102% of your Stryd Auto-Calculated Critical Power. Your goal for this 4 x 5:00 session is to start conservatively the first 5:00 repeat around 95% of your threshold power (Critical Power in this example) and progress the second and third repeat from 95-102% of your CP. After your last repeat run an easy cool down.

EXAMPLE 2: **EASY + STRIDES**

"Strides" are defined as short bursts of faster running to get your body used to running at a higher intensity. Your goal for strides should be to start a bit above your CP and practice running at a fast speed without straining. After a brief warm up, you will run 30 seconds repeats with an easy 1-minute recovery. After you have completed the number of repetitions, cool down with an easy segment of running.

EXAMPLE 3: **LONG RUN**

The long run is a main staple in training and is your longest continuous effort in the training week. The goal for this run is to practice extending duration and increasing your time spent running. Over the course of the training plan this run will build in duration and slightly vary in intensity.

My threshold power (CP) is barely getting better?

Runners who train with a power-based training plan often come up with the question above. To answer the question, you need to understand how software is used to calculate your threshold power (or CP).

The effects of your workouts diminish over time. The excellent race you ran in the previous year no longer contributes to your fitness today. It typically makes sense to track about 90 days of data. Therefore, older runs are no longer considered.

Likewise, software will use your hardest runs that still matter (i.e., within the last 90 days) to calculate your threshold power. For example, if you ran a 10K race in the beginning of your training cycle, your regular workouts are unlikely to be at a higher intensity. The software will therefore not calculate a higher threshold power for you until you do a run where you beat a previous effort from the past three months. However, your fitness is likely improving if you stick with the training plan, you just haven't "proved" it yet.

Some training plans have regular time trials built in that will give you a chance to beat your power target, or have you test yourself in a 5K or 10K race. If you exceed your personal best from the last 90 days, your threshold power (CP) will increase, and your plan adapts.

For example, the blue line in Ron's power curve below is the result of a recent run. The white line models Ron's capability for any duration up to 90 minutes. If you feel that you are fitter than software is giving you credit for, you can do a "jack-up" or boost workout. The goal is then to run the power according to the model (the white line in the graph) in a workout. The blue line then shifts locally to the white line. A hard jack-up workout in the range of 20 to 50 minutes contributes the most to the improvement of your CP. If you "beat" the modeled ability, your CP goes up.

A maximum effort workout improves your power duration curve. Your CP will adapt if it also shows a better fitness. In that case, your future workouts will be adjusted so that the power levels with which you must run the workouts increase.

Since a maximum effort puts a lot of stress on your system and increase risk of injury, you cannot do a "jack-up" training often. Most plans will have you do such a workout every 4 to 8 weeks to avoid problems.

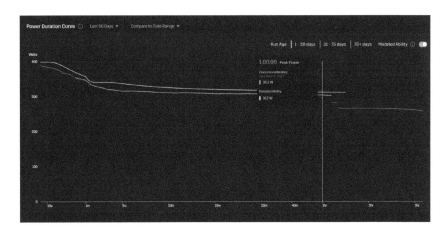

5.10 From Target Power to race time. Why factor 1.04?

Again this chapter is a direct result of a question from one of our readers. He is an enthusiastic user of power meters and asked us how he could calculate his race time from the Target Power for a specific distance?

We have a very nice and simple formula that answers this question. With this formula, everyone can calculate the race time very easily. The formula gives the race time in ideal conditions, so a fast course without differences in altitude and without any wind. If you also want to know how much slower you run in non-ideal conditions (such as hills, wind or forest trails), things become a bit more complicated and you will have to use our calculator or our spreadsheet with the complete running model.

Below we first provide some background information and then we present our simple formula and a handy table of race times with different values for your (specific) power. If you want to dive into the details, you should read on, because in the second part of this chapter we explain how we derived the formula.

How much power can you sustain?

You will be aware of our running model, which we have described in the chapter The running model. The figure in that chapter shows the basic concept of the model, namely that the power of the human engine P must be equal to the sum of the powers required to surmount the running resistance P_r, the air resistance P_a and the climbing resistance P_c.

When you train more and better, the power of your human engine P will increase so you will have more power available to overcome the 3 resistances, allowing you to run faster. As everyone will understand, your running power

P depends on the duration of the effort and therefore the distance: at a longer distance you have to slow down somewhat so your running power is lower. This is described in the chapter The power-time relationship.

You need to know your Functional Treshold Power (FTP). This is the power that you can sustain for 60 minutes. Author Hans, for example, has an FTP of 256 Watts, the race calculator (or at choice chapter The power-time relationship) tells him that during a Half Marathon race he should maintain a Target Power of 243 Watts. So our big question now becomes: what will be the HM-race time for Hans at 243 Watts?

Simple formula to calculate your race time

Our formula is super simple: to calculate your time T (in seconds) you should just enter your Target Power (TP, in Watts), your body weight m (in kg) and the distance d (in meters).

$$T = 1.04 * d / (TP/m)$$

For the example of author Hans, d = 21098 m, TP = 243 Watts and m = 58 kg. The result of the formula is 5,237 seconds or 1:27:17.
This time matches well with the performances of Hans on the half marathon.

Based on the formula, we have compiled the table below that gives a good picture of the achievable times as a function of the specific target power (TP/m in Watts/kg). So from now on you can very easily calculate or read off your attainable time from the table when you know with which specific target power (TP/m) you want to run the race!

The results of the table correspond very well with practice. In deriving the formula, we have of course neglected some aspects (in particular the individual running economy and the individual air resistance), which means that deviations of 1 or 2% can occur in individual cases. This is explained at the end of this chapter. There we will discuss exactly how the formula works.

The formula applies, as stated before, only for ideal conditions, so a fast course without altitude differences and in windless weather. In the table we have finally indicated the extreme values for the specific power in red. These values are outside of the (current) human physiological limits.

How to calculate race-time from target power by rule of thumb?					
Target Power	10K	15K	10EM	Half Mar.	Marathon
(Watts/kg)	(hr:min:sec)	(hr:min:sec)	(hr:min:sec)	(hr:min:sec)	(hr:min:sec)
2.00	1:26:40	2:10:00	2:19:27	3:02:51	6:05:41
2.25	1:17:02	1:55:33	2:03:57	2:42:32	5:25:03
2.50	1:09:20	1:44:00	1:51:33	2:26:17	4:52:33
2.75	1:03:02	1:34:33	1:41:25	2:12:59	4:25:57
3.00	0:57:47	1:26:40	1:32:58	2:01:54	4:03:48
3.25	0:53:20	1:20:00	1:25:49	1:52:31	3:45:02
3.50	0:49:31	1:14:17	1:19:41	1:44:29	3:28:58
3.75	0:46:13	1:09:20	1:14:22	1:37:31	3:15:02
4.00	0:43:20	1:05:00	1:09:43	1:31:25	3:02:51
4.25	0:40:47	1:01:11	1:05:37	1:26:03	2:52:05
4.50	0:38:31	0:57:47	1:01:59	1:21:16	2:42:32
4.75	0:36:29	0:54:44	0:58:43	1:16:59	2:33:58
5.00	0:34:40	0:52:00	0:55:47	1:13:08	2:26:17
5.25	0:33:01	0:49:31	0:53:07	1:09:39	2:19:19
5.50	0:31:31	0:47:16	0:50:42	1:06:29	2:12:59
5.75	0:30:09	0:45:13	0:48:30	1:03:36	2:07:12
6.00	0:28:53	0:43:20	0:46:29	1:00:57	2:01:54
6.25	0:27:44	0:41:36	0:44:37	0:58:31	1:57:01
6.50	0:26:40	0:40:00	0:42:54	0:56:16	1:52:31
6.75	0:25:41	0:38:31	0:41:19	0:54:11	1:48:21
Notes:					
1. Running economy (ECOR) and air-resistance have been approximated					
2. Calculations are for ideal conditions (no wind and no hills)					
3. For exact calculations use spreadsheet of TSOR					
4. Red marked powers are beyond (current) physiological limits					

Backgrounds / theory

In the chapter The running model we have discussed the theory of our running model. The full equation is shown in the box below.

$$P = cmv+0.5\rho c_d A(v+v_w)^2 v+(i/100)mgv$$

The full equation is rather complex: it is a third-degree with many parameters that are needed to describe the impact of the different aspects. We have programmed an Excel spreadsheet that solves this third-degree equation and can be used to calculate the exact impact of all parameters. Interested readers can request this Excel from us, but we expect most runners will prefer the simple formula that we present in this chapter.

The simple formula is based on some assumptions. First that there are no hills in the course ($i = 0$), so the third part of the equation becomes zero and therefore disappears. Second there is no wind ($v_w = 0$), making the second part of the comparison a lot easier.

What remains with these simplifications is the mathematical equation:
$P = ECOR*m*v+0.5*\rho*c_d A*v^3$.
We then divide the left and right parts of the equation by the body weight m, so we get:
$P/m = ECOR*v+0.5*\rho*c_d A*v^3/m$.

The specific power P/m is the most important parameter that determines the quality of the runners. World best runners have a specific power of more than 6 Watts/kg, while recreational runners may have a value around 3 Watts/kg.

This difference in specific power is the most important reason why world best runners run so fast. You can easily see that by neglecting the air-resistance, the equation then simplifies to $P/m = ECOR*v$, so the speed is directly proportional to P/m. Next it should be remarked that world best runners usually run more economically than recreational runners, so their ECOR (Energy Cost Of Running in kJ/kg/km) is also lower.

The relationship between the specific power, ECOR and running speed is (globally and simplified) shown in the table below. Note the differences in ECOR. This is because less talented athletes have a lower metabolic efficiency.

Level	FTP/CP	ECOR	v
	(Watts/kg)	(kJ/kg/km)	(m/s)
World Best	6.4	0.93	6.88
National	5.0	0.98	5.10
Running Enthusiast	4.0	1.01	3.96
Fitness Runner	3.0	1.03	2.91
Poor	2.0	1.06	1.89

We next looked at the second part of the equation, the air-resistance. It appears that this has more or less the opposite effect: world best runners run faster (so v is higher) and therefore face a much higher air-resistance than fitness runners (due to their 'own' running wind).

The relationship between the running speed of the different runners and the air-resistance (in Watts/kg, we have used a body weight of 60 kg) and the air-resistance/v (in kJ/kg/ km) is shown in the table below.

Level	v	air-resistance	air-resistance/v
	(m/s)	(Watts/kg)	(kJ/kg/km)
World Best	6.88	0.79	0.11
National	5.10	0.32	0.06
Running Enthusiast	3.96	0.15	0.04
Fitness Runner	2.91	0.06	0.02
Poor	1.89	0.02	0.01

So we clearly see the aforementioned effect: world best runners have to deal with much more air- resistance (from their 'own' wind) than fitness runners.

Next, we simplify the running formula once more to P/m = (ECOR+ air-resistance/v)*v.
The air-resistance/v factor indicates the specific energy consumption of the air-resistance (similarly to ECOR in kJ/kg/km).
In the table below we give the end result, which shows that the sum of

ECOR and air-resistance/v has more or less a fixed value of 1.04-1.05 for most runners.

Level	FTP/CP (Watts/kg)	ECOR (kJ/kg/km)	air-resistance/v (kJ/kg/km)	ECOR+air-res./v (kJ/kg/km)
World Best	6.4	0.93	0.11	1.04
National	5.0	0.98	0.06	1.04
Running Enthusiast	4.0	1.01	0.04	1.05
Fitness Runner	3.0	1.03	0.02	1.05
Poor	2.0	1.06	0.01	1.07

The formula to calculate race time from Target Power

As explained above in the simple formula the value of 1.04 can be used. So that the running speed at a specific Power (P) can be calculated with the formula: $v = P/m/1.04$.

To determine the time T in seconds, for a specific power we only have to divide the distance d (m) by the speed v (m/s), so that the end result becomes:
$T = 1.04*d/(P/m)$.

5.11 Training with the magic predictor of your marathon time: Yasso 800s

Koen de Jong uses the Yasso 800s method for his marathon training and asked us if we knew the method and could calculate the required power to run the Yasso intervals. We answered in the affirmative to both questions and in this chapter we explain the method and how to calculate the required power to run the intervals.

What is the Yasso 800s?

The Yasso 800s was created by Bart Yasso, the Chief Running Officer of the American magazine Runner's World. Bart Yasso has been inducted into the Running USA Hall of Champions and is referred to in America as the 'Mayor of Running'. He has raced on all 7 continents and has won the U.S. Duathlon Championship in 1987.

His method is very simple and consists of running a number of intervals over 800 meters. The trick is that you have to make sure that your time over the 800 meters (in minutes and seconds) is equal to your marathon goal time (in hours and minutes). So if you run (or want to run) a marathon in 3 hours you have to run the 800 meters in 3 minutes. How simple can it be?

The structure of the workout is also very simple:
• Warm-up for 10 minutes (gentle jogging, exercises and possibly some 100 meter strides to get used to the speed)
• 800 meter interval at the converted pace (so 3 minutes for a marathon time of 3 hours)
• Recovery during the same time as the interval (so 3 minutes in the example)
• Repetitions: in the beginning 3 or 4 times, expand to finally 10 times
• Cooling down for 5 or 10 minutes, including exercises/stretching.

And voilà, you're done!

Bart Yasso recommends doing this training 1 time a week. The method is very popular and also successful. It is recommended to do the other parts of a full marathon training during the rest of the week, especially the long endurance runs, the recovery runs and the pace training.

What power should you use for the Yasso 800s?

In the table on the next page we have worked out some examples. The first column shows the (desired) marathon goal time.
In the second column we have determined the corresponding marathon power with the formula: **Watts/kg = speed in m/s*1.04**. In the chapter From Target Power to race time. Why factor 1.04? we showed that this gives a very good approach for most runners.

The third column shows the time for the Yasso 800s in minutes and seconds, which as mentioned is equal to the marathon time in hours and minutes.
In the fourth column, the required power for the 800 meters is calculated (with the same formula).
In the fifth column we have finally calculated how much extra power you have

to use during the 800 meters compared to your marathon power. This always turns out to be 13.76% with this method.

Marathon time (h:min:sec)	Marathon power (Watts/kg)	Yasso 800 (min:sec)	Yasso power (Watts/kg)	Extra power (%)
2:00:00	6.09	2:00	6.93	13.76
2:15:00	5.42	2:15	6.16	13.76
2:30:00	4.88	2:30	5.55	13.76
2:45:00	4.43	2:45	5.04	13.76
3:00:00	4.06	3:00	4.62	13.76
3:15:00	3.75	3:15	4.27	13.76
3:30:00	3.48	3:30	3.96	13.76
3:45:00	3.25	3:45	3.70	13.76
4:00:00	3.05	4:00	3.47	13.76
4:15:00	2.87	4:15	3.26	13.76
4:30:00	2.71	4:30	3.08	13.76

Critical analysis of the Yasso 800s

At first glance, this method seems too simple to be true. You would think: how is it possible to base a marathon time on intervals over 800 meters and vice versa?

Still, there's something in it. Of course, you run slower as the distance increases. In this book we have shown that for most people the speed decreases by 5% when the distance doubles. Now of course there are people with a particularly good endurance, but when you cannot run an 800 meter interval in 4 minutes you can forget about running a marathon in 3 hours. No matter how good your stamina is! That there is a more or less fixed relationship between the 800 meters and the marathon time is therefore not entirely surprising, although this will not be exactly the same for everyone.

At its core, the Yasso 800s is 'just' an interval workout where the pace of the intervals is not determined by your coach, but by your desired marathon time. In earlier chapters, we have already shown that interval training is an important building block to become a better runner. With the Yasso 800s, the pace of your intervals is therefore adjusted to your level, in this case by the marathon time you can or want to run. If you don't reach that level, you'll have to adjust the pace of your workouts and the expectations for the marathon....

Intervals make you a better runner

Many performance-oriented runners train at least once a week at their club on the athletics track. Traditionally, your trainer often bases the schedules for interval training on your 10K race time. On another day in the week, some longer intervals, accelerations or hills in the workout on the road or in the forest are on the program.

The reason is that with intervals you can train at high intensity. It improves your base speed. The goal can also be to train your various energy systems (youhave four!) or to get your body used to lactate acid. Because recovery is built in between intervals, these types of training are less stressful as a race.

800 meter intervals at 109%?

In the chapter Power-based interval training, we gave the table below for the required power as a function of the distance of the intervals. For intervals of 800 meters, we indicated that you have to run it at 109% of your FTP (the power that you can maintain for 1 hour).

Interval distance [m]	Percentage FTP [%]
2000	100%
1600	102%
1200	104%
1000	107%
800	109%
600	114%
400	120%
200	126%
100	133%

The fact that you see the percentages increase quite a bit at short interval distances is caused by the fact that your anaerobic energy systems provide extra energy there. See the chapter Your four energy systems. Your anaerobic fuel supply is very limited. You can therefore only keep these high powers and speeds up for a short time.

What about the Yasso 800s? Do you also run it on 109% of your FTP? We have calculated that for the examples given, see the table below. The first 2 columns are the same as in the first table, but in the third column we have calculated the FTP that is equivalent to the marathon time. In the fourth column we have finally calculated the required power for the 800s as a percentage of your FTP. Because your marathon power is relatively lower compared to your FTP at slower marathon times, you see that the percentage with which you have to run the 800 meters slowly decreases.

Marathon time (h:min:sec)	Marathon power (Watts/kg)	FTP (Watts/kg)	Yasso %FTP (%)
2:00:00	6.09	6.40	108
2:15:00	5.42	5.73	107
2:30:00	4.88	5.20	107
2:45:00	4.43	4.76	106
3:00:00	4.06	4.39	105
3:15:00	3.75	4.07	105
3:30:00	3.48	3.80	104
3:45:00	3.25	3.57	104
4:00:00	3.05	3.36	103
4:15:00	2.87	3.16	103
4:30:00	2.71	2.98	103

The result of these calculations is that the elite runners with the Yasso method have to run almost at 109% of their FTP, but that for slower runners the percentage drops to order 103%. The workout is therefore less stressful for them, especially since the recovery time at Yasso is rather long (after all, as long as the interval itself, so 4 minutes if you run a marathon in 4 minutes).

Our conclusion is that the Yasso 800s is a great method to determine the pace for your intervals on your individual level, based on your marathon time. For slower runners, the pace seems to be a bit too slow and the recovery time is also a bit too long. However, it does seem a bit dubious to us to predict your marathon time from your Yasso 800s interval times. Keep in mind that in the marathon you may 'hit the wall' and your stamina may be better or less than average.

5.12 Strong winds

A big storm swept over the Netherlands on Thursday March 11, 2021. "Heavy wind gusts of 80 to 90 kilometers per hour occur throughout the country, and in the north and west from 100 to 110 kilometers per hour. The peak falls in the last hours of the morning and at the beginning of the afternoon. The storm is expected to move away around 2 p.m." Ron went out at 11:13 am for a workout of about 10K.

Ron decided to run his workout at the time that Evert was at his most powerful. A great opportunity to check whether the Stryd running power meter measures the Air Power correctly.

Wind Port

A power meter for a bike calculates the power from the force you put on the pedals. When the wind blows harder, you must pedal harder, and you see the wattage increase immediately if you maintain your speed. A Stryd foot pod determines power with precision instruments (IMUs) in the foot pod on the laces of your running shoe that convert motion into a power number.

Stryd uses a 'wind port' for the air-resistance. This measurement method is known from the flow theory that is also used, for example, in the aircraft industry. In fact, it measures air pressure differences.

Stryd uses the term Air Power and defines it as follows "Air Power represents the extra power needed to overcome air-resistance". The power shown on your watch is total power, the power needed to move forward and the extra power to overcome wind resistance. Due to limitations in technology, Stryd's

Air Power never shows negative power (which is the case when the tailwind velocity exceeds your running speed). This is a disadvantage but as can be read in chapter Wind from all directions the impact of tailwind is smaller than of headwind.

The workout on flat terrain yielded the following graph of the airpower. On the horizontal axis the distance (in kilometers) is shown and on the vertical axis the Air Power (in Watts). The graph is from Golden Cheetah as Stryd Power-Center presents the data differently.

The wind speed was 50 to 60 km/h with gusts up to 100 km/h. During the run, there was some shelter of buildings and trees but on the other hand, in some section the wind had free rein. At times Air Power was more than 100 Watts! For running, that's a lot. It feels as if you are running up a steep slope. It even yielded a new 5-seconds value and 10-seconds maximum value for Ron's power duration curve: 459 Watts and 391 Watts respectively.

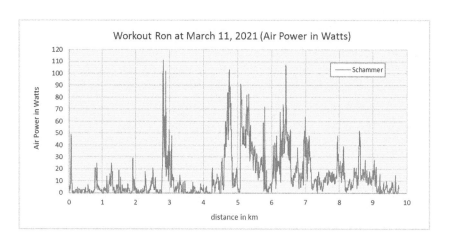

Wind is always detrimental for your time

The problem with wind is that it always is a disadvantage. One reason is that even cross wind together with the running wind produces headwind. There are more angles where the wind produces a disadvantage then there are angles where wind brings an advantage.

We've explained that in more detail in the chapter Wind from all directions. In the graph above with the Air Power you can see that there were segments with virtually no drag. Then you run easily. As on a flat treadmill.

For a workout, a strong wind is not a bad thing. You can turn it into a fartlek training where you keep pace the same and change. Or you can run intervals at a slower pace but at the same effort. In a race, on the other hand, you are unlikely to run a personal best with wind unless you are running a point-to-point course like the Boston Marathon with westerly winds. By running smartly, however, you can limit time lost and optimize race performance. For example, you can look for a group of runners and "hide" between them from the wind, or you can look for areas less exposed to wind.

Ron (80 kg) ran the workout with an average of 263 Watts. The Air Power averaged 5.58%. This is about double the percentage of a day with light wind. The big storm therefore caused an average disadvantage of 10 seconds per kilometer. That's seven minutes in a marathon.

A running power meter with wind measurement offers you the opportunity to optimize your performance. You do this by ignoring pace and focus on power while running. You keep running your power target as calculated in advance, avoiding exceeding your power target when the wind picks up. In the graph you see that the wind at times swallows up 40% of your power. If you slow down and keep effort the same, you will have the best possible performance under the circumstances, although it is slower than in a marathon in better conditions.

As the wind gusts and is never constant, in practice you may not be able to keep power exactly constant. The more constant you keep your wattages, the better. To achieve this you can set a 3 seconds or 10 seconds average for the power metric to smooth data on your watch.

Finally, we give the map from Garmin Connect to show how the wind blew during the workout. Every 500 meters Ron's Garmin gives a lap.

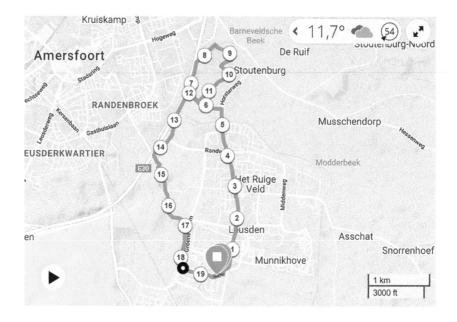

With our model we have calculated the impact. Ron had mostly a cross head wind or cross tail wind. If we enter the average pace of Ron (5:37/km) and a wind speed of 54 km/h (15 m/s, wind force 7) in our model, we get the following results for air-resistance + running resistance = total running power:

- head wind angled (45°) = 370 Watts total running power
- tail wind angled (45°) = 194 Watts total running power

The fact that the average Air Power for this workout 263 Watts is, seems very plausible.

5.13 North Sea Half Marathon: the impact of the wind

More than 10,000 participants in a half marathon on the North Sea beaches and dunes had to face wind up to 50 km/h on a 7-kilometer stretch of beach. The elite athletes decided to waste as little power as possible. In a closed pack they kept each other out of the wind. Once they reached the dunes, the race actually started and each picked up the personal fastest pace.

Windspeed of 50 km/h is perfect to illustrate the impact of wind on your running performance.

In a closed pack the runners battled against frontwind force 6 on the beach.

An example: Niels

Master athlete Niels ran this half marathon with a Stryd with wind port. Niels was so kind to provide us his fit-file with running data for analyses.

"Once protected from the wind in the dunes, I could easily run my own speed. On the beach, exposed to the full force of the wind, this was impossible. Unfortunately I started in the back of a group that was somewhat slow for me. In this group of about 20 runners I could often hide behind someone else, but not all the time. Also I ran short parts in front of the group.", Niels explained.

Was it really so bad to start at the back? We think this was not bad at all and running in a pack is a must under these circumstances.

In the table below we have summarized the average data of the performance of Niels and included the road map as well. Upto the turning point, after the first 7 kilometers, the runners battled a fierce wind running on the beach at low tide. After leaving the beach the course went through the dunes with a lot of undulations.

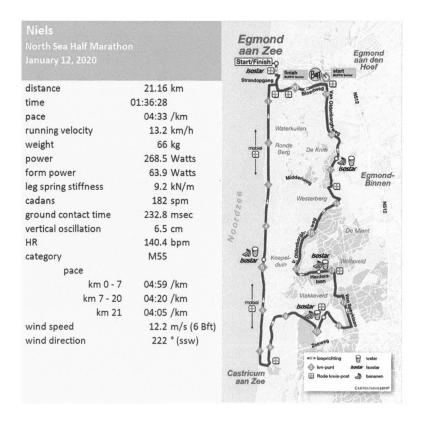

Niels
North Sea Half Marathon
January 12, 2020

distance	21.16 km
time	01:36:28
pace	04:33 /km
running velocity	13.2 km/h
weight	66 kg
power	268.5 Watts
form power	63.9 Watts
leg spring stiffness	9.2 kN/m
cadans	182 spm
ground contact time	232.8 msec
vertical oscillation	6.5 cm
HR	140.4 bpm
category	M55
pace	
km 0 - 7	04:59 /km
km 7 - 20	04:20 /km
km 21	04:05 /km
wind speed	12.2 m/s (6 Bft)
wind direction	222 ° (ssw)

How about Air Power?

We have read Niels' database into the Golden Cheetah analysis program. For every second we got the wattage that Niels (66 kg) needed to surmount the wind.

The first 7 kilometers, his Air Power averaged around 40 Watts, with peaks of 70 Watts and more. From the 19-K point onwards, Niels faced a crosswind which cost him around 20 Watts Air Power.

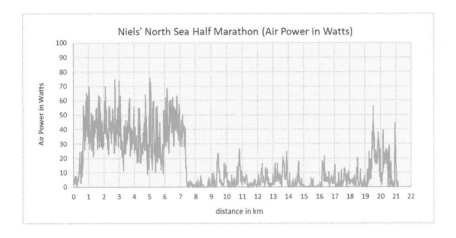

Stryd's current technology measures head- and crosswinds without problems. Tailwinds also work fine untill the tailwind speed exceeds running speed. You can see that in the graphs as Air Power is never a negative number even though the wind was very strong. In practice, this is not a big problem as tailwind is less beneficial than the cost of running against the wind.

Run at constant Total Power

We explained earlier that your performance is best if you run at constant power. That is why you need to run slower uphill and faster downhill. The same principle applies to running against the wind. Facing a headwind, you need to slow down and hide as much as possible in a group. With a tailwind you need to run faster.

The graph below shows the Total Power and the Air Power of Niels during the half marathon. The first kilometer was downhill and, as he said, Niels could not run his own pace. From the 2K-point onwards his Total Power was around 270 Watts. He managed to maintain this wattage throughout the race with a slight increase during the final kilometer to the finish. Well done, Niels!

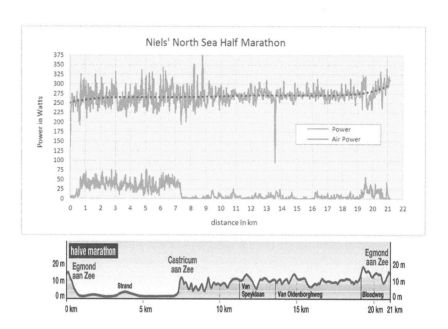

Run slower with headwind and faster at tailwind

On the beach, a significant percentage of Niels' Total Power was needed to overcome air-resistance. Consequently, less power was available for moving forward and his pace dropped as shown in the next graph. On the beach his pace was near 5:00/km. In the dunes, with the same Total Power, his pace was 4:20/km. Near the finish Niels sprinted with a pace of 4:05/km. His average pace was 4:33/km. Finish time 1:36:28.

The y-axis in the next figure shows what percentage of Total Power was needed to overcome the wind. We show his running velocity on the same scale (in km/h). On the beach Niels ran 12 km/h. In the dunes almost 14 km/h and in the final sprint around 15 km/h.

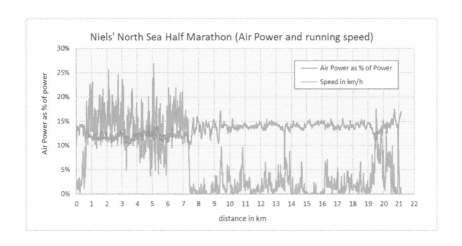

Niels' North Sea Half Marathon (Air Power and running speed)

How much time lost due to the wind?

Niels finishing time was 1:36:28. His wattage was 270 Watts on average. What would Niels's time have been in ideal conditions, so no wind and on a hard and even road? In the case of Niels (half marathon, 66 kg, 270 Watts) this would have been 1:29:24 according to our model. Consequently, for Niels, it turned out to be 7 minutes slower than a half marathon with ideal conditions.

How big was the advantage of running in the pack?

Due to the wind Niels lost about 40 Watts on the beach. The question is how much Niels benefited from running in the pack there? The wind direction was southwest, at around 40° angle against the runners, with an average wind speed of 12.2 m/s (44 km/h).

With our running model we calculated that in these conditions 84 Watts is required to overcome the air-resistance. Thanks to his running power meter we know that on average Niels needed around 40 Watts. Consequently, the average Air Power was 52% less than theory. The difference can largely be explained from the advantage of running in the pack.

In cyling, similar percentages are known from riding in a pack. Of course the wind speed may also have been higher or lower at times. Finally, we draw your attention to the outliers above 70 Watts in the graph, which in our opinion show the moments when Niels ran in front of the group. At these moments he did not have the full advantage of the pack, so his Air Power was near the theoretical calculated value. Note that, even the person in the lead of a pack still has a slight advantage when running in a pack (which is why Eliot Kipchoge had pacers running behind him (as well as in front) during his successful sub-2 hours marathon).

All in all, we believe this case is a near-perfect example of the validity of the concept of Air Power and the usefullness of the Stryd in these conditions. We conclude with a final remark from runner Niels himself: "it is almost unbelievable how accurate and usefull Stryd is". Very usefull indeed in windy countries.

5.14 Dubai Marathon

The winning time of 20-year-old Ethiopian Olika Adugna Bikila was not really a record for the 2020 Standard Chartered Dubai Marathon. Usually the elite athletes run a lot faster in Dubai than 2:06:15, Dubai has one of the fastest marathons in the world. However, the fact that 11 athletes ran faster than 2:07 is a remarkable result and most probably a record!

An astonishing group of 11 elite athletes sprinted towards the finish together, all finishing within 19 seconds. 10 out of 11 ran or matched their personal best. What magic was in the air in Dubai?

The leading group of 24 athletes passed the half marathon in 1:02:43 (photo courtesy: Standard Chartered Dubai Marathon)

Favorable conditions

On Friday morning, February 23rd 2020, the gun fired at 6 p.m. for the elite athletes. It was still dark, dawn was an hour later. The Dubai marathon course is perfectly flat and asphalted. The athletes ran back and forth on the coastal road, facing a gentle headwind during the first half marathon and enjoying a bit of tailwind during the second half. The temperature was 20°C (cool for Dubai conditions) and the humidity was good at 73%.

There was a lot at stake. 100,000 US Dollars was the prize money for the winner. Number 2 got less, 40,000 US Dollars. Number 10 still received 2,500 US Dollars. At the finish line number 11 was only 19 seconds slower than the winner and went home with a commemorative medal....

A strong elite field

Traditionally many Ethiopians participate in Dubai. Of the first twenty finishers, eighteen were from this country. Most of them are member of one of the professional Ethiopian athletic clubs who run all over the world for prize money.

The table shows the data of the first twenty finishers in the men's race. Fourteen of them are marked in yellow. These athletes ran a PB or had their marathon debut. Two others equalled their PB and are indicated in green. It is striking that some PB's have been sharpened with minutes, even when set at a recent date, 2019 or 2018.

We know that the first eleven ran with the fast Nike Vaporfly Next% shoes. This shoe is on the market since mid-2019. Presumably the previous PB was also set with this shoe or with predecessor Nike Vaporfly 4%, so the shoe cannot be the only reason for this remarkable result.

place Dubai marathon	name	finish time	prize money (US$)	former best (PB)	when?	where?
1	Adugna Bikila, Olika (ETH)	2:06:15	$100,000	debut		
2	Kiprono Kiptanui, Eric (KEN)	2:06:17	$40,000	debut		
3	Abeje Ayana, Tsedat (ETH)	2:06:18	$20,000	2:06:36	2019	Sevilla (ESP)
4	Tesfaye Anbessa, Lencho (ETH)	2:06:18	$10,000	2:10:49	2019	Venezia (ITA)
5	Atnafu Zerihun, Yitayal (ETH)	2:06:21	$5,000	2:07:00	2018	Paris (FRA)
6	Adane Amsalu, Yihunilign (ETH)	2:06:22	$4,500	2:09:11	2019	Beppu (JP)
7	Bantie Dessie, Aychew (ETH)	2:06:23	$4,000	2:06:23	2019	Paris (FRA)
8	Tura Abdiwak, Seifu (ETH)	2:06:26	$3,500	2:04:44	2018	Dubai (UAE)
9	Deso Gelmisa, Chalu (ETH)	2:06:29	$3,000	2:09:08	2019	Porto (POR)
10	Hailu Bekele, Zewudu (ETH)	2:06:31	$2,500	debut		
11	Yerssie Eskezia, Beshah (ETH)	2:06:34	$0	2:08:37	2019	Chuncheon (KOR)
12	Bacha Regasa, Zelalem (BRN)	2:07:09	$0	2:09:16	2018	Seoul (KOR)
13	Yihunie Derseh, Balew (ETH)	2:07:26	$0	2:07:22	2019	Chuncheon (KOR)
14	Fufa Nigassa, Abdi (ETH)	2:07:51	$0	2:09:24	2018	Shanghai (CHN)
15	Abate Deme, Tadu (ETH)	2:08:54	$0	2:06:13	2019	Amsterdam (NED)
16	Asefa Bedada, Belay (ETH)	2:09:11	$0	2:06:39	2019	Sevilla (ESP)
17	Gebremariam, Tigabu (ETH)	2:10:15	$0	2:19:14	2012	Roma (ITA)
18	Getachew Yizengaw, Limenih (ETH)	2:10:26	$0	2:06:49	2014	Paris (FRA)
19	Gashahun Tilahun, Abe (ETH)	2:11:02	$0	debut		
20	Faye Tiki, Dejene (ETH)	2:12:08	$0	2:16:14	2013	Casablanca (MAR)

The race

At half marathon the leading group consisted of no less than 24 athletes. They passed in 1:02:43. The average pace in the first half was 2:59/km, exactly the same as in the second half. A steady pace is already a key to success, as is well-known.

The second success factor was that the runners understood the advantage of running in a pack. This reduces the air-resistance, decreases the energy cost of running, and results in faster finish times.

Possibly the runners didn't expect to be all together in the last few kilometers, so they had to sprint for the 100,000 US Dollars. It turned out that the fastest sprinter was a marathon debutant. The following table clearly shows that the pack really maintained a perfect pace at every 5-km point.

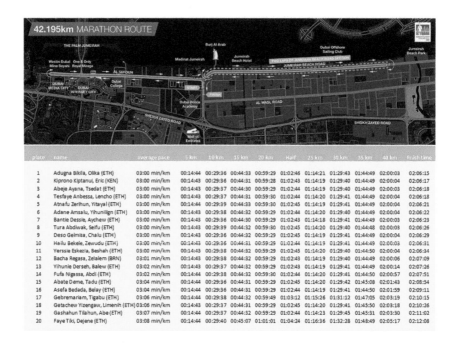

place	name	average pace	5 km	10 km	15 km	20 km	Half	25 km	30 km	35 km	40 km	finish time
1	Adugna Bikila, Olika (ETH)	03:00 min/km	00:14:44	00:29:36	00:44:33	00:59:29	01:02:46	01:14:21	01:29:43	01:44:49	02:00:03	02:06:15
2	Kiprono Kiptanui, Eric (KEN)	03:00 min/km	00:14:43	00:29:36	00:44:31	00:59:28	01:02:43	01:14:19	01:29:40	01:44:49	02:00:04	02:06:17
3	Abeje Ayana, Tsedat (ETH)	03:00 min/km	00:14:43	00:29:37	00:44:30	00:59:29	01:02:44	01:14:19	01:29:40	01:44:49	02:00:03	02:06:18
4	Tesfaye Anbessa, Lencho (ETH)	03:00 min/km	00:14:43	00:29:37	00:44:31	00:59:30	01:02:44	01:14:20	01:29:41	01:44:49	02:00:04	02:06:18
5	Atnafu Zerihun, Yitayal (ETH)	03:00 min/km	00:14:44	00:29:39	00:44:33	00:59:30	01:02:45	01:14:19	01:29:41	01:44:49	02:00:04	02:06:21
6	Adane Amsalu, Yihunilign (ETH)	03:00 min/km	00:14:43	00:29:38	00:44:32	00:59:29	01:02:44	01:14:20	01:29:40	01:44:49	02:00:04	02:06:22
7	Bantie Dessie, Aychew (ETH)	03:00 min/km	00:14:43	00:29:36	00:44:30	00:59:29	01:02:43	01:14:18	01:29:41	01:44:49	02:00:03	02:06:23
8	Tura Abdiwak, Seifu (ETH)	03:00 min/km	00:14:43	00:29:39	00:44:32	00:59:30	01:02:45	01:14:20	01:29:40	01:44:48	02:00:03	02:06:26
9	Deso Gelmisa, Chalu (ETH)	03:00 min/km	00:14:43	00:29:36	00:44:32	00:59:29	01:02:45	01:14:19	01:29:41	01:44:49	02:00:04	02:06:29
10	Hailu Bekele, Zewudu (ETH)	03:00 min/km	00:14:43	00:29:36	00:44:31	00:59:25	01:02:44	01:14:19	01:29:41	01:44:49	02:00:03	02:06:31
11	Yerssie Eskezia, Beshah (ETH)	03:00 min/km	00:14:43	00:29:38	00:44:32	00:59:29	01:02:45	01:14:20	01:29:40	01:44:50	02:00:04	02:06:34
12	Bacha Regasa, Zelalem (BRN)	03:01 min/km	00:14:43	00:29:38	00:44:32	00:59:29	01:02:44	01:14:19	01:29:40	01:44:49	02:00:06	02:07:09
13	Yihunie Derseh, Balew (ETH)	03:02 min/km	00:14:43	00:29:37	00:44:32	00:59:29	01:02:43	01:14:19	01:29:41	01:44:49	02:00:14	02:07:26
14	Fufa Nigassa, Abdi (ETH)	03:02 min/km	00:14:44	00:29:38	00:44:32	00:59:30	01:02:44	01:14:20	01:29:41	01:44:50	02:00:57	02:07:51
15	Abate Deme, Tadu (ETH)	03:04 min/km	00:14:44	00:29:36	00:44:31	00:59:29	01:02:45	01:14:20	01:29:42	01:45:08	02:01:43	02:08:54
16	Asefa Bedada, Belay (ETH)	03:04 min/km	00:14:44	00:29:36	00:44:31	00:59:29	01:02:44	01:14:19	01:29:42	01:44:50	02:01:59	02:09:11
17	Gebremariam, Tigabu (ETH)	03:06 min/km	00:14:43	00:29:38	00:44:32	00:59:49	01:03:12	01:15:26	01:31:12	01:47:05	02:03:19	02:10:15
18	Getachew Yizengaw, Limenih (ETH)	03:06 min/km	00:14:43	00:29:37	00:44:31	00:59:29	01:02:45	01:14:20	01:29:41	01:45:50	02:03:18	02:10:26
19	Gashahun Tilahun, Abe (ETH)	03:07 min/km	00:14:44	00:29:37	00:44:32	00:59:29	01:02:44	01:14:23	01:29:45	01:45:31	02:03:30	02:11:02
20	Faye Tiki, Dejene (ETH)	03:08 min/km	00:14:44	00:29:40	00:45:07	01:01:01	01:04:24	01:16:36	01:32:28	01:48:49	02:05:17	02:12:08

Two success factors: the shoes and running in the pack

From the data, we calculated the advantages of the shoes and running in the pack.
We assumed that the total running resistance was 2% lower thanks to the
shoes. For running in the pack, we have assumed a $c_d A$ air-resistance factor of
0.20 m². Running alone, the air-resistance factor is 0.24 m². For our calculations we used the conditions in Dubai (temperature, air pressure and wind).
We calculated with a bodyweight of 56 kg. Of course this will differ for these
athletes, but is used for the ease of the analysis:

With our running model we calculated that running alone and on normal
shoes, the power of the first 11 in Dubai should have been 331 Watts to reach
the 2:06:15 finishing time. This complies to a Functional Threshold Power
(FTP) of 6.20 Watts/kg. Earlier we explained that the maximum power of the
world records in running complies to a FTP of 6.4 Watts/kg, so the Dubai
finishers did not quite reach the level of Eliud Kipchoge.

Next, we calculated that the power required to reach the 2:06:15 on normal shoes
while running in a pack is 327 Watts only, equivalent to a FTP of 6.13 Watts/kg.

Finally, we calculated the power while running in a pack and on shoes with a 2% advantage: the result is 321 Watts, equivalent to a FTP 6.01 Watts/kg. In the chapter Super shoes is elaborated what advantage you can expect from such shoes.

So we conclude that both the shoes and running in the pack gave the runners a significant edge: they needed some 11 Watts (equivalent to a FTP of 0.19 Watts/kg) less to reach the finishing time of 2:06:15.

We have also calculated the impact of the shoes and running in the pack on the equivalent finishing times of the runners.

The results are that an athlete with a power of 321 Watts would finish the marathon in 2:09:44, while running alone and on standard shoes. The same runner would finish in 2:08:22, while running alone but on the Nike's Vaporfly Next% shoes. Finally, the same runner would finish in 2:06:15, while running in the pack and on the new shoes.

Conclusions

The shoes are not cheap, cannot be afforded by everyone but have proven to be a great help.

Everyone can run in a pack. In the big races you can join pacers who run at a fixed pace to a predetermined finish time. Almost without exception, these pacers run with a large group followers. You can easily join them, thus lowering your air-resistance, and sharpen your PB with one or more minutes.

5.15 Justin Gatlin:
100 meters in 9.45 seconds

We frequently discuss the worldwide quest of runners, coaches and running scientists for options to optimize the running performance through reducing the air-resistance. Cyclists and speed-skaters have been doing this for a long time already by developing optimal aerodynamic conditions (clothing, frames, body position, streamlining, drafting).

This chapter focuses on a spectacular demonstration of the impact of the air-resistance. Back in 2011 American sprinter Justin Gatlin ran the 100 meters in a sensational time of 9.45. He managed to do this during a special race organized by the Japanese TV-show Kasupe!. They had arranged that he was assisted by a tailwind provided by huge fans (capable of blowing wind at 32 km/h).

Consequently, Gatlin ran faster than the present-day world record of Usain Bolt (9.58), although he had never run faster than 9.95 seconds in regular races in the 2011 season. Apparently, the tailwind gave him a nett advantage of no less than 0.5 seconds!

In this chapter, we calculate how high advantage in the air-resistance has been to explain the result.

Theory

According to the fundamental laws of physics, the power required to surmount the air-resistance P_a is determined by the density of the air ϱ (in kg/m³) the air-resistance factor c_dA (in m²), the running speed v (in m/s) and the wind speed v_w (in m/s), as equation: $\mathbf{P_a = 0.5\varrho c_d A(v+v_w)^2 v}$

The figure below shows the air-resistance as a function of running speed v at the standard conditions (temperature 20°C, air-pressure 1013 mbar, so ϱ = 1.205 kg/m³, c_dA = 0.24 m², no wind, so v_w = 0 m/s). At Gatlin's speed (38.1 km/h) the air-resistance at the standard conditions equals a staggering 171 Watts.

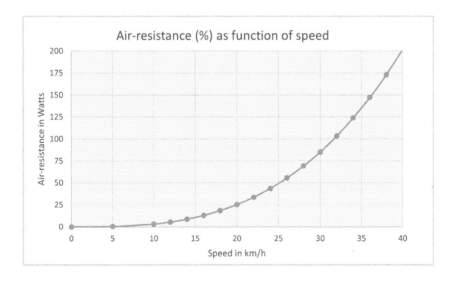

How big was the advantage of the tail wind?

This question cannot be easily answered as we do not know exactly how high the wind speed was. YouTube tells us that the speed in the fans was 32 km/h, but a large part of this wind will have been lost to the ambient air. It seems obvious that the real tailwind that Gatlin experienced was much lower.

We have estimated this tailwind by using the power balance: $P_t = P_a + P_r$. So, we have assumed that the total power P_t of Gatlin remained the same. Without tail wind, this power enabled him to run 9.95, with tailwind the same power enabled him to run 9.45.

In the case without tail wind, his speed was 10.05 m/s, so his P_B must have been 10.05*79*0.98 = 778 Watts (body weight 79 kg and ECOR 0.98 kJ/kg/km). At this speed his P_a was equal to 147 Watts, so apparently his P_t was 925 Watts.

In the case with tailwind, his speed was higher (10.58 m/s). Consequently, his P_r was 819 Watts which is 41 Watts higher than in the case without wind. So, we conclude that the air-resistance must have been 41 Watts lower as a result of the tailwind.

Next, we have used the formula above to calculate at which wind speed the air-resistance would be reduced by 41 Watts. This results in a tailwind speed of 5.8 km/h or only 18% of the speed of the fans. The results are summarized in the table below.

Justin Gatlin		tail wind	no wind	
	time	9.45	9.95	seconds
	speed	10.58	10.05	m/s
P_a		105	147	Watts
P_r		819	778	Watts
P_t		924	925	Watts

We note that this is a simplified calculation as we have neglected the power required for the acceleration in the first part of the race. Actually, sprinters use a significant part of their power for this acceleration. As Gatlin obtained a higher speed with the tail wind, this means that he also will have used somewhat more power for the acceleration. When we taken this into account, the real tail wind speed will be higher than the above calculated 18%.

How fast could Justin Gatlin have run without any air-resistance?

This can be easily calculated as in this case P_a is equal to 0. This situation could occur when running on a treadmill or in a long wind tunnel with an air speed of slightly more than 10 m/s. In such cases Gatlin could use his total running power of 925 Watts for the running resistance P_r.

The result thus becomes a speed of 925/79/0.98 = 11.95 m/s or a 100 meters time of 8.4 seconds! This calculation is also simplified as we did not take into account the power required for the acceleration in the first part of the race.

In our book 'The Secret of Running' we have calculated a similar time for Usain Bolt. On the one hand his P_t is larger than that of Gatlin and he was faster in normal races. On the other hand Bolt was heavier, so the air-resistance was relatively smaller in his case. The formula shows that the air-resistance is independent of the body weight, which means heavy runners have a small advantage.

5.16 Headwind versus inclines

Each year we see heroic rides of the Tour de France professional cyclists who hit the wall as they climb the Alpe d'Huez or a similarly challenging mountain. Puffing and sweating they labor uphill, while their pace drops to a pedestrian level. This is most inspiring to the fans, as these arduous efforts are almost unimaginable.

Most of us do not have the opportunity of running the climb to the Alpe d'Huez on a daily basis for training. However, some of us do have to face some pretty nasty weather, including strong wind or even storms. We all have experienced that a strong head wind can be very tough indeed. At severe wind gusts, you almost come to a complete standstill! We were wondering which is actually tougher: running Alpe d'Huez or battling a high windspeed of 60 km/h?

How tough is the effort of running uphill at Alpe d'Huez?

In chapter How much time do hills take? we have calculated the attainable speed uphill the Alpe d'Huez as a function of the FTP. The result for our Marathon Man (70 kg, running the marathon in 3:30) is that he could maintain a speed of 9.2 km/h with his FTP of 3.67 Watt/kg. At a flat course, Marathon Man can attain a speed of 13.1 km/h with his FTP. So, we have taken the speed reduction to 9.2 km/h as the criterion for how tough running uphill the Alpe d'Huez really is. Next, we compared this with the speed reduction because of a headwind to see which effort is the toughest.

Climbing the official running course Alpe d'Huez (length 13.8 km, altitude difference - with steady incline - 1,020 meters)

How tough is running into a head wind?

Earlier we have calculated the attainable speed of Marathon Man as a function of the wind speed. From those data, we can conclude that his speed drops to 9.2 km/h at a head wind with a speed of 43 km/h. This is equivalent to windspeed of 50 km/h, a strong breeze. So, we conclude that - perhaps surprisingly - running into a headwind with a windspeed of 60 km/h is tougher than running Alpe d'Huez!

Which wind speeds and gradients are equally tough?

We have also taken a more general approach to the topic by investigating at which conditions the air-resistance equals the climbing resistance:

$$P_a = 0.5 \varrho c_d A (v+v_w)^2 v$$

$$P_c = (i/100) m g v \eta$$

To simplify matters, we made some assumptions. We have used the standard conditions (m = 70 kg, ϱ = 1.226 kg/m³, $c_d A$ = 0.24 m²) and we have set speed to 10 km/h. In these conditions, the figure below gives the wind speeds and gradients that fulfill the criterion that the wind resistance and the climbing resistance are equal.

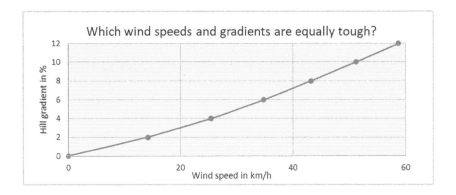

In summary, we conclude that a strong headwind can provide the same resistance as a steep gradient. A head wind of 25 km/h matches the resistance of a 4% gradient! So, training in flat countries is not necessarily easier than training in mountainous areas. However, the wind conditions are far less stable and predictable. At times you almost come to a standstill in a headwind and at times you could be flying because of a tailwind. All in all, the training conditions change continuously. The impact of such a workout can, therefore, not easily be compared with that of a continuous climb.

5.17 Faster over seven hills with Nike Vaporfly Next%

The fastest 15K course in the world is in the Netherlands: The Seven Hills Run. In 2019, Ethiopian Letesenbet Gidey ran her world record (44:20) here. A year earlier Joshua Cheptegei from Uganda ran the 15K in 41:10, setting the present world record. Over the years, more world records have been run here.

Objective

In 2021 Ron ran for fun but had also a mission. He wanted to see if the Nike Vaporfly Next% brought the promised benefit. The conditions in Nijmegen were ideal, a temperature of 9°C (which felt like 7°C) and a barely noticeable wind. Ron has run almost all editions of the Seven Hills Run and knows the course like the back of his hand.

The intention was to show that those expensive super shoes produce faster times for all runners. Not just for elite runners, as is often claimed. This notion is because tests with this new type of shoes are often done with fast athletes that easily run a 5K in less than 16 minutes.

1:15:05

Ron used the Stryd race calculator to get a reliable forecast of the achievable time in advance. This race calculator is part of the Stryd web platform. You can load the FIT or GPX file of the course into the race power calculator, no problem for Ron to get such a file as he ran the course many times before. The race power calculator takes the profile of the course into account (shown in gray in the figure on the next page). The race power calculator combines the course profile with critical power and power duration curve.

The Stryd ecosystem keeps track of the environmental conditions of all your training runs. Therefore, the race power calculator knows under what conditions you trained. You can enter the temperature, humidity, and elevation on race day so that the predicted power and race time are adjusted. For example, if you train at sea level but your race is on 1,600 meters in Colorado, you will be running at a slower pace (lower air-resistance but less oxygen in the air).

Based on the training data, the course details, and the environmental conditions, the race power calculator estimated a time of 1:15:05 for Ron and recommended a target power of 289 Watts (orange line in the figure). Ron weighs 80 kg. A person with lower weight can take the hills faster, the race power calculator takes this aspect into account as well.

You will notice that the power target remains constant for the event, but that pace fluctuates due to the undulations. That makes sense. By keeping effort for both uphill and downhill segment as constant as possible, aiming for 289 Watts, Ron can set his fastest possible race time for this race day. This means that the pace uphill will be slower than expected by most runners. And downhill requires some serious acceleration. The blue line shows the changes in pace.

During the race there is no need to have continuous attention to your real-time power. It is sufficient to check every now and then your running watch (which you have linked with your Stryd) whether you are still running (within a range)

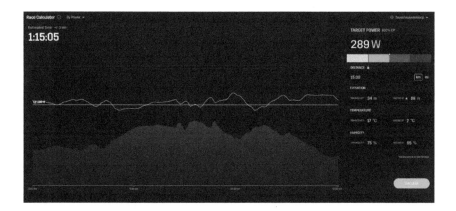

at 289 Watts. Some watches can show you average power every desired interval, e.g. half kilometer or mile, which helps you understand whether or not your last interval was at the right power target. In two spots, the course had a descent that was too steep to keep the target power. Note that Ron only needed to worry about power. Other metrics like pace are not important during the race.

1:12:32

Ron knew he could exceed his target of 289 Watts. 289 Watts was based on workouts run with regular shoes such as the Adidas Ultraboost 21, Brooks Glycerin 19, and HOKA One One Bondi 7.

Nike Zoom Vaporfly Next% promises a 4% advantage. Ron increased his power target to 300 Watts and finished with an average power of 302 Watts (+4.5% compared to 289 Watts) and a time of 1:12:32 (-3.4% compared to 1:15:05). When we take the impact of the hills into account, it seems likely that the Nike super shoes do what they promise, even for average runners!

How was Ron able to increase his power target, though? FTP or Critical Power reflect the power of the human engine and therefore does NOT increase if you wear fast super shoes. Running power is currently not a direct measurement but calculated based on motion by an algorithm. As the new shoes increase your efficiency, Ron could add 4% the 289 Watts target. His oxygen consumption was the same as if he would have run at a lower target with his regular training shoes. Because of the increased efficiency the Vaporfly race time is 3-4% faster.

Nice response

In the evening we got a nice response from a runner who had owned a Stryd for just a week and who contacted us before the race:"That was an excellent tip! I followed your advice. The first 8 kms were slower than in 2018, but I was able to speed up in in the last 4 kilometers downhill. Really fun, and 50 seconds faster than my PB! Running on power really is ideal for those hills! And likely for other runs as well, I'm pleasantly surprised!"

If you just got started with a power meter, the race power calculator cannot yet reliably forecast an achievable time. That is why we helped this runner. We based our advice on a time that he had run in the recent past: 26:00 for a 5K. The calculator on our website TheSecretofRunning.com calculates that this is equivalent to a VO_2 max of 42.69 ml O_2/min/kg and a functional threshold power (FTP) of 3.06 Watts/kg. With a body weight 63.5 kg, this runner can maintain 194 Watts for an hour.

What race time this runner could achieve on a flat course of 15K can be determined with our calculator: 1:24:14. Knowing this time the table below from the chapter The power-time relationship helps calculate a power target:

Power ratio with time	
Time (minutes)	% FTP (%)
10 (= VO_2 max)	113
20	108
40	103
60 (= FTP)	100
120	95
240	91
300	89

If you can sustain 194 Watts for an hour, it is a reasonable that you can run 15K in about 1:24:14 with a 190 Watts target, 98% of his FTP. That was our advice. Our friend achieved 1:25:52 with a power average of 193 Watts. Considering the hills, the prediction was near perfect!

5.18 The Energy Cost of Running (ECOR) up and down hills

In several chapters of this book we discussed the Energy Cost of Running (ECOR). We have shown that on a level and hard course and neglecting air-resistance, the ECOR is typically 0.98 kJ/kg/km. Of course, this number will not be the same for everyone. It depends on the running style and every runner should try to optimize this in order to reduce his ECOR. Obviously, a running power meter gives us the tool to do this as can calculate our ECOR on a daily basis:

ECOR (in kJ/kg/km) = Specific power (in Watts/kg) divided by the speed (in m/s)

Generally, it is believed that the ECOR of highly efficient elite runners could be some 5% lower and the ECOR of inefficient joggers could be some 10% higher than the typical value of 0.98 kJ/kg/km.

The impact of hills on the ECOR according to theory

As a result of gravity, the ECOR is increased uphill and decreased downhill. This effect can theoretically be calculated as a function of the gradient i (in %) by the formula:

ECOR= 0.98+ i/100*9.81*(45.6+1.16*i)/100

We have calculated the ECOR in accordance with this formula, the results are shown in the below figure. The figure show clearly that hills do indeed have a big impact on the ECOR!

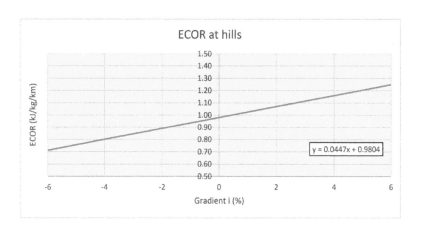

The impact of hills on the ECOR in practice
The impact of hills on the ECOR in practice

We did an experiment to validate these theoretical calculations. Both authors (Hans and Ron) ran uphill and downhill a nearby hill with a length of 1 km and a gradient of 3.7% (so the total altitude difference was 37 meters). We ran 2 times uphill and 2 times downhill, with recovery in between. We used our Stryd foot pod to monitor our power and we tried to run at our FTP-level, which is the amount of power that you can maintain for 1 hour.

At the date of the experiment the FTP of Hans was 245 Watts or 4.22 Watts/kg and for Ron these data were 300 Watts and 3.75 Watts/kg. The results are shown in the table on the next page.

Hans (58 kg)	Time (min:sec)	Speed (m/s)	Power (Watts)	(Watts/kg)	ECOR (kJ/kg/km)	HR (bpm)	Stride length (m)	Cadence (spm)	Vert. osci. (cm)	GCT (msec)	FP (Watts)	FP/P (%)	LSS (kN/m)
Uphill 1	04:33	3.66	245	4.22	1.15	160	1.19	187	7.6	225	51	21%	8
Downhill 1	03:22	4.95	230	3.97	0.80	157	1.54	195	8.9	198	58	25%	10
Uphill 2	04:28	3.73	258	4.45	1.19	155	1.19	191	7.4	229	52	20%	8
Downhill 2	03:25	4.88	234	4.03	0.83	152	1.53	193	9.0	202	60	26%	10
Ron (80 kg)													
Uphill 1	05:12	3.21	306.1	3.83	1.19	137	1.10	174	6.3	283	68.3	22%	9.0
Downhill 1	03:46	4.42	280.8	3.51	0.79	135	1.42	186	6.6	236	72.8	26%	9.5
Uphill 2	05:11	3.22	312.1	3.90	1.21	137	1.11	175	6.2	280	69.6	22%	9.1
Downhill 2	03:46	4.42	289.9	3.62	0.82	133	1.44	185	6.7	236	75.2	26%	9.5

As can be seen from the table, we did not quite manage to maintain our FTP downhill. As other experienced runners will confirm, this is due to the fact that stride length and cadence limit the possible speed downhill. The table also confirms the obvious facts that uphill stride length, vertical oscillation, FP and LSS are reduced. Downhill the reverse is the case.

The most important result is that the data clearly confirm that the ECOR is substantially higher uphill and substantially lower downhill. As a matter of fact the actual values are remarkably close to theory. We were quite impressed by the fact that the power data represented the impact of the hill so accurately and in accordance with theory. Hats off for the running power meter development guys!

ECOR experiment on hill with i = 3.7%	Theory	Hans	Ron
Uphill	1.15	1.15-1.19	1.19-1.21
Downhill	0.81	0.80-0.83	0.79-0.82

5.19 The physiology of Eliud Kipchoge and his 'Breaking2' pacers

The English sponsor and owner of the INEOS group Sir Jim Ratcliffe honours Eliud Kipchoge at his phenomenal 1:59:40 in Vienna.

On October 12th, 2019, Eliud Kipchoge succeeded in Vienna (Austria) in his mission to break the 2 hours barrier for the marathon. Enthusiasts from all over the world were glued to the screen to admire his groundbreaking result with a fantastic 1:59:40. Eliud and his team of 41 pacers and coaching staff managed a unique and historic achievement.

We read a scientific paper[1] that Andrew M. Jones published on the physiological studies carried out with the team of Eliud and his pacers. Alex Hutchinson[2] of Sweat Science summarized and analyzed the results of the paper. We also used the data from the study to evaluate and review Eliud's performance in the context of our universal running model.

You know that your marathon race time depends on the conditions. A flat

[1] Physiological demands of running at 2-hour marathon race pace, Andrew M. Jones et al., Journal of Applied Physiology, 18 February 2021, https://doi.org/10.1152/japplphysiol.00647.2020
[2] We Now Have the Lab Data on Nike's Breaking2 Runners, Alex Hutchinson, Sweat Science outsideonline.com, 6 November 2020 https://www.outsideonline.com/health/training-performance/nike-breaking2-runners-lab-data/

course is better than a course with undulations. Cold weather is better than hot. No wind is better than running in windy conditions. Obviously, Eliud's team selected a course that would be a closest to ideal as possible. Even under ideal conditions, success still depends on the following factors:

1. VO_2 max (i.e. the power of your human engine)
2. Stamina (i.e. the percentage of VO_2 max/power you can maintain during the marathon)
3. Running efficiency (this is your energy consumption per km, depends on running style, physique and also your shoes)
4. Air-resistance (this is lower if you are running behind pacers or in a group)

The first 3 parameters have been analyzed in-depth by academic research. Sixteen top runners of Nike's 'Breaking2' marathon project were tested in the laboratory and on the track. The runners were mainly from Kenya and Ethiopia and had an average PB of 1:00:04 on the half marathon and 2:08:40 on the full marathon (the marathon average is lower as Zersenay Tadese had not yet run a fast marathon). The data is anonymized, so we do not know the individual data of Eliud Kipchoge. The oxygen consumption was measured in a classical way, not just to determine the VO_2 max, but also during test runs with a speed of 21.1 km/h.

VO_2 max

The most striking result of the study is that the average VO_2 max of these elite runners was "only" 71 ml/kg/min. A higher value would be expected for these elite runners. The maximum measured value was 84 ml/kg/min, so we assume that this was Eliud Kipchoge. You can find several websites[3] that give an overview of the highest values of VO_2 max ever measured. A summary in the table below:

Highest VO₂ max measured (ml/kg/min)	
Oskar Svendson	97.5
Greg Lemond	92.5
Bjorn Daehlie	90.0
Miguel Indurain	88.0
Chris Froome	84.6
Lance Armstrong	84.0
Jim Ryun	81.0

[3] World Best VO2max Scores, topendsports.com, https://www.topendsports.com/testing/records/vo2max.htm

The table shows that the value of 84 ml/kg/min is high, but not exceptional. Occasionally even higher values have been measured, especially for cyclists and cross-country skiers. Oskar Svendson's VO$_2$ max is known to be exceptionally high, but at the expense of metabolic efficiency (which was better than the typical value of 25%). Earlier we have shown that you can calculate power P of your human engine using the following formula:

P (in Watts/kg) = VO$_2$ max (in ml/kg/min)*0.0815

This means that the power calculation for Eliud Kipchoge is 84*0.0815 = 6.84 Watts/kg.

This power level can only be sustained for the duration of the VO$_2$ max test, i.e., 10 minutes. You can compare this power with the top values of professional cyclists who sometimes reach similar values during short climbs of 10 minutes. Because Eliud weighs 56 kg, his total power is 6.84*56 = 383 Watts, sustainable for 10 minutes only.

Endurance

The second special (albeit perhaps slightly less striking) result of the study is that these elite athletes have exceptional stamina. They turned out to be able to run the marathon at 88% of their VO$_2$ max! This is really very special, as normal 84% is already a good value and many runners don't manage more than 75-80% of their VO$_2$ max during the marathon. At 88%, Eliud ran the marathon with a power of 0.88*6.84 = 6.02 Watts/kg or 0.88*383 = 337 Watts.

Running efficiency/energy consumption

The third special (albeit slightly less striking) result of the study is that these elite athletes have a very efficient running style. They use very little oxygen and therefore energy per km. The average oxygen consumption was only 191 ml/kg/km. This corresponds to a net energy consumption (ECOR) of 0.93 kJ/kg/km. For normal runners a value of 0.98 kJ/kg/km is already nice and values up to 1.10 kJ/kg/km are common for untrained. Where you can compare the VO$_2$ max with the power of your human engine you can compare the energy consumption with the gas mileage. These elite runners are very economical and can therefore run faster with their VO$_2$ max!

Super shoes

In Vienna Eliud also ran with the latest Nike Alphafly shoes. According to Nike they are the fastest shoes ever made. This will certainly also have had a positive effect on the energy consumption (some 4% lower as explained in chapter Super shoes in this book).

The aerodynamic resistance

Reducing aerodynamic drag was definitely a key success factor at the super performance in Vienna. Eliud received help from five teams, each with seven pacers that alternately kept Eliud out of the wind. The team of pacers included several world champions.

The pacers ran in a surprising V-formation. The captain of the team ran in front of Eliud, with two pacers to the left and right in front of the captain. Left and right behind Eliud were the sixth and seventh pacers. They also used a pacer car, which drove 15 meters in front of the group, so that the airflow was optimal.

From the car, laser lines were projected on the road surface as an aid for the pacers to maintain the right pace and position. Guiding lines were drawn on the road surface. The picture nicely shows the formation with Eliud in the middle and the next team of pacers ready for the next relaying.

View of the exchange of the pacers. Eliud Kipchoge runs in white.

We calculated that all these measures had the effect of reducing air resistance by 33%. If Eliud would have run alone, without pacers, we estimate his c_dA air resistance value at 0.24 m², given his stature. In Vienna, his c_dA value was only 0.16 m². With our model, we calculated that the energy consumption for the air resistance was therefore only 0.06 kJ/kg/km (i.e. only 6% of the energy consumption for the running movement itself).

Reversed V-formation

At the previous record attempt in Monza (2017, marathon time 2:00:25), the pacers ran in a diamond formation in front of Eliud Kipchoge. Since, more than a hundred formations were analyzed using computer simulations by aerodynamics specialist Robby Ketchell of AvantCourse (USA) and later by professor Bert Blocken. The most optimal formations from this analysis were tested in Blocken's wind tunnel at Eindhoven University of Technology in The Netherlands.

Against everyone's expectations, the formation of a reversed V with five pacers in front of the athlete and two behind him, proposed by Robby Ketchell, turned out to be the most optimal variant. This formation was feasible thanks to the frequent relays with fresh pacers.

Conclusions

The research of the Nike 'Breaking2' marathon team provided interesting insights into the physiological data of Eliud Kipchoge and his pacers. The most important findings are:

1. VO_2 max of 84, this is high (the corresponding power is 6.84 Watts/kg)
2. Endurance is exceptionally high, 88% of VO_2 max during 2 hours! The result is that Eliud could run the marathon with a power of 337 Watts.
3. Running efficiency is very high, oxygen consumption 191 ml/kg/km and energy consumption (ECOR) 0.93 kJ/kg/km
4. Air resistance is 33% lower due to pacers, the energy consumption to overcome air-resistance is only 0.06 kJ/kg/km

We have entered this data (and the other data such as temperature, air pressure, altitude and wind speed) into our running model. The model calculates a speed of 21.2 km/h, very close to the speed of the 21.1 km/h Eliud sustained during the entire marathon.

5.20 Tested: COROS Pace 2

The favorably priced new COROS Pace 2 packs a host of features. 'The lightest GPS watch on the market, weighing just 29 grams' with Eliud Kipchoge as ambassador. We've used the watch daily during a period. In this chapter we show the pros and cons of the COROS Pace 2.

We compared the COROS Pace 2 with a Garmin Fenix 6X, a 93-gram high end multisport watch, and with the Stryd running power meter. One may think you should not compare a Volkswagen with a BMW. On the contrary, a comparison with a top model is interesting. How does a cheaper watch stack up against a top-of-the line competitor?

GPS and wind

Both Garmin and COROS were tested using the American GPS and Russian GLONASS systems.

With COROS you can choose between three combinations of satellite navigation networks:
1. GPS + Japanese QZSS + GLONASS,
2. or GPS + QZSS + Chinese BeiDou,
3. or GPS + QZSS.

Garmin offers three other choices:
1. GPS,
2. or GPS + GLONASS,
3. or GPS + European Galileo.

The more satellites a watch "sees", the more accurate it is in terms of positioning. GPS watches calculate distance and speed by monitoring your position over time. Therefore, the better the watch can determine your position, the better metrics it will offer for pace and distance.

The figure on the next page shows the test result of running 7 times 1,450 meters around the complex of our athletics club Altis. After 7 laps, COROS recorded a distance of 10.01 km, and the Garmin 10.04 km. A difference of 30 meters, negligible for satellite positioning systems.

The figure below also that both watches have a considerable spread in the width of the registered course. The COROS is on the left (yellow lines) and the Garmin on the right (colored lines). At the start of each round we gave a lap. The 500 meters markers of the COROS (set by programming autolap to 500 meters) are closer together than Garmin's. In this limited test, COROS is fractionally better than Garmin.

During the same workout we compared COROS Running Power with Stryd Power. According to the COROS, we ran with an average of 243 Watts. Stryd has an average of 247 Watts, of which 2% is due to the wind. If we zoom in, we can see why. The power on the individual laps differs with headwind and tailwind. The wind blew with 19 km/h, not a strong wind but some impact on the effort required to run a certain pace.

You optimize performance by running with even power. In the figure from the Garmin you can see that the pace was slightly lower with headwind (mostly blue) and slightly higher (mostly green with some orange) with tailwind. Because COROS does not take air-resistance into account Stryd beats COROS Running Power.

Running on athletics track

Both watches have the option to improve accuracy on an athletics track. The bends of a track are though for GPS watches to get right. Like Garmin, COROS offers a 'Track Run' activity. In both cases, it is advised to start with a minimum of four laps on the track to calibrate the watch. We did this. COROS indicated after just one lap that the track had been recognized. We ran with both watches twice 2,000 meters (5 laps) in lane 1. Hereafter another 2,000 meters was run twice, but with the watches in the regular 'Run' mode.

The next figure shows that 'Track Run' is a powerful solution for the annoying deviation of GPS watches on an athletics track. COROS in yellow and 'track run', on the top left in the figure. Garmin in colors, also with 'track run' on the bottom left. Both watches do well. The fact that Garmin came twice at exactly 2,000 meters is excellent. The figure also shows examples of five laps run with the normal activity 'Run'. It incorrectly suggests that the track has been used over a large width while we only ran in lane one. It is a close finish, but Garmin wins with 'Run on track'.

How to measure the right distance on track

A certified running track in only 400 meters in one specific line in lane one. If you deviate from this ideal line, you will run more than 400 meters. Watches that have a track mode assume you always run the perfect line in the lane chosen. If you are not running exactly 30 cm from the inner edge of lane 1, or in a different lane, the total distance will be off.

The average power of Stryd and COROS Running Power were about the same at the track tests, differing just by 1 Watt and once by 2 Watts.

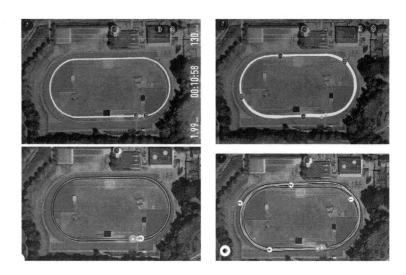

COROS with Stryd

We don't have comments on the combined use of the COROS Pace 2 and a Stryd: it works perfect. COROS offer a host of options for power data fields, just like Garmin. We like the 10 seconds average wattage, which is a good compromise between responsiveness and stability. Cyclists will recognize that power meters vary from second to second. By using average over a number of seconds, the value smoothens and can be easier to use on flat terrain.

COROS Running Power

The COROS Pace 2 can also provide running power without a Stryd foot pod. For this purpose, the watch combines GPS, motion sensor, and barometer data.

Garmin Running Power and Polar Running Power do the same. The difference with Garmin and Polar is that COROS, just like Stryd, calculates the net power as we use in this book and is common in cycling. Garmin and Polar produce an approximately 25% higher gross power value. This is explained in the chapter Why Polar (and Garmin) running power values differ 25%?.

If you add the COROS Pod, COROS offers extra running metrics, like Stryd and what Garmin offers in combination with the HRM-Run chest strap. Stryd does not provide (or need) heart rate information. The Garmin chest strap does measure heart rate. Garmin provides no information about Form Power and Leg Spring Stiffness.

The COROS Pod must be attached to the waistband of running pants or shorts on your back. It feels as if the pod can easily be lost, but that has not happened. While it is secure, attached to the laces of the shoe would feel more secure.

We have two comments about COROS Running Power during an interval workout.

1. Although the watch was ready, during the warming-up in the figure below (COROS left, Stryd right), the GPS was not yet accurate enough to determine power. Apparently, the watch got still too little satellite information. As a result, the watch continued to beep and vibrate because power was either too high or too low. The figure on the next page (the first 2 km) shows this clearly. A nice feature is that the COROS screen turns red when the wattage is too high and blue when the wattage is too low. Hot and cold! This is like the Stryd Workout app for Garmin watches.

2. The workout consisted of 5 blocks of 500 meters with higher power. At the transitions you can see in the graphs some delay in the values. GPS technology has inherent disadvantages over a foot pod attached to the shoe. GPS location data varies quite a bit, which means that watches use an algorithm to smooth out errors to get the best possible data. Therefore, the watch needs a bit of time to calculate a reliable power number whereas Stryd is more immediate. During interval training (or any other change in pace or terrain), it is more difficult to hit the right power target immediately with COROS. The consequence is that you are likely to start too fast,

and need to adjust after 30 seconds to get power just right. Stryd power is immediately at the right value, making Stryd easier to use.

In the figure the yellow lines of Stryd are perpendicular. Enlarged you can see this better than in the picture below. With short strides (60-100 meters) this is especially important for the evaluation afterwards whether or not the workout was done at the right power.

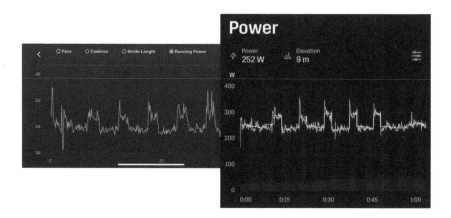

Hills

We also tested both running power meters in hills. We ran a one-kilometer ascent and equally long descent. COROS uses an accurate barometer to determine incline and adjust running power. Stryd also has a barometer and combines this with data from accelerometers (IMU's) in several directions. Uphill COROS comes close to the Stryd values albeit with some delay. Downhill power from COROS is 8-9 Watts lower (3%). This can partly be explained by the (little) headwind during the run that Stryd considers. The Stryd power meter is better than COROS Running Power for hills.

The total distance of this run with hills was 18.35 km according to COROS. The Garmin watch configured to use Stryd data for pace and distance recorded 18.40 km. A negligible difference.

Training with power

The COROS app lets you create power-based workouts in the app that can be transferred to the watch. If you often repeat the same workout, this works well as the workout is stored in a library. COROS also offers a set of training plans in their own app.

The COROS system integrates with TrainingPeaks. This is great as you can purchase any plan you like from a long list of coaches.
The COROS watches have a workout feature, guiding you through a workout. This is similar to the Stryd Workout app. The watch works well, and the experience is great.

COROS does not import power-based workouts from the Stryd ecosystem. That means that if you own a Stryd and want to take advantage of Stryd's free power-based plans or their workout builder, you need to rebuild the workout in COROS Training Hub, launched in December 2021. Intensity types you can select are Heart Rate, Pace, Cadence and of course Power.

The Team View functionality of the COROS training hub gives coaches the possibility to invite athletes and create their own team with instant access to their athlete's fatigue, and plan completion for quick decision making. Coaches also have the possibility to access each athlete's profile, analyze workouts, schedule training, and communicate through the platform. This is more or less similar to what Stryd offers.

Conclusion

COROS Pace 2 with a Stryd foot pod is a good purchase. We recommend Stryd over the (cheaper) COROS Pod.

The Garmin Fenix 6X is bigger and looks more robust than the cheaper COROS Pace 2. Garmin combined with a Stryd offers additional options over COROS, such as navigation. Not a feature the average runner uses a lot. More expensive COROS models offer navigation as well, but not yet as slick as GPS watches from specialist Garmin. All in all, the expensive Garmin beats the COROS Pace 2 in this test. And a Stryd for is the best experience to run with power.

We do compare a Volkswagen with a BMW. The choice is a matter of taste, price, and what features matter to runners. The internals are quite similar, and Garmin offers cheaper models that combine well with a Stryd. The cheapest compatible Garmin is currently sold at nearly the price as the COROS Pace 2. In this comparison, the COROS Pace 2 offers more value for money.

Wrist-based heart rate measurements are poor in both cases. If you want to use heart rate data for training, you better get a chest strap. The Garmin HRM-Run chest strap provides a lot of extra running metrics and (with some watches) also Garmin Running Power (based on GPS and wrist motion).

We did not expect the white nylon strap of the COROS to stay white. But it did! We did always rinse after a workout. The COROS Pace 2 is also available with silicone straps which makes the watch slightly heavier but will likely keep its color for longer. The battery life of 30 hours of exercising is what makes COROS stand out as compared to similarly priced watch. The Garmin Fenix 6X can last 60 hours, but a higher cost in money spent and weight. Battery life, of course, depends on functions used.

5.21 Why native Polar (and Garmin) running power values are 25-30% too high?

The breakthrough of running power meters has led to a fierce competition between suppliers. Stryd was the first to introduce running power with their motion sensor technology (housed in a foot pod) in 2016.

Since then, apps have been developed using GPS, barometer and accelerators in smart phones, for example Power2Run, or as I/Q app Running Power Estimator for Garmin watches. Power2Run app was launched for Apple watch using GPS and barometric data. Meanwhile, Garmin and Polar, the traditional suppliers of running watches, have developed their own running power technology based on the sensors in their watches. Strava supports running power data form all major brands (Garmin, Polar, Coros, Apple, Suunto and Stryd) from September 2021. In addition to other power information about your running performance, Strava provides subscribers, for example, a powermap of their workout.

While this competition is all good news to the running community as it leads to lower cost and better quality, runners and in particular triathletes have noticed one particularly confusing and troublesome aspect: the power numbers of some suppliers are much higher (around 25-30%) than the power numbers of other suppliers and the power numbers in cycling. Why is this so and what do the numbers mean?

We have tested many power meters and we have also found these differences. We have had some intensive discussions[1] on the reasons and the interpretation of the results. Unlike power meters for cycling, running power meters do not measure forces but accelerations and use an algorithm to calculate power. In this chapter we first discuss the background of the force plate method that developers use to calibrate their algorithm.

[1] Among others, dr. Jussi Peltonen of Polar and Kun Li of Stryd

On top of the force plates, some calibrate their power meters with metabolic data of VO$_2$ of test runners. As a result their numbers match the universal theory of sports from our books. Finally, we will explain why there are differences in power meter numbers and how this should be interpreted.

Hans van Dijk & Ron van Megen | The Secret of Running

The use of force plates

Some developers calibrate their running power algorithm with force plates. These record the horizontal and vertical components of the force applied by the runner. The horizontal force and the vertical force (minus the body weight) can be integrated to calculate the horizontal and vertical velocities and finally the kinetic and potential energies. The running power can then be determined from the total of the kinetic and potential energies divided by time.

The method to calculate power from measurements has first been described in 1975[2]. In our discussions with developers we observed the method is well documented and can stand the test of scientific scrutiny.

---

[2] G.A. Cavagna, Force platforms as ergometers, Journal of Applied Physiology, 1975 (39), 1, pp. 174-179

Force plates, power cranks and pedals

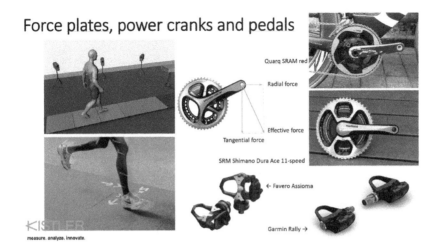

Quarq SRAM red

Radial force

Effective force

Tangential force

SRM Shimano Dura Ace 11-speed

← Favero Assioma

Garmin Rally →

KISTLER
measure. analyze. innovate.

The universal theory of sports

In the chapter The running model, we explained our universal model of sports and the applications for running and cycling. In short, the model is based on the concept of the 'human engine', which consists mainly of the heart-lung system and the muscles.

The capacity of the human engine can be described in terms of the maximum oxygen uptake (VO_2 max in ml O_2/kg/min) or in terms of Functional Threshold Power (FTP, in Watts/kg). As the oxygen is used to produce energy from the transfer of glycogen and fatty acids, there is a direct relationship between FTP and VO_2:

FTP = 0.072*VO_2 max

Referring to the chapter The FTP (CP60), the above formula is based on the following standard literature values: energy production through O_2 19.55 kJ/l, gross metabolic efficiency 25% and power duration factor FTP (60 minutes) and VO_2 max (10 minutes) is 0.88.

In our book The Secret of Running we have presented many results of the validity of this model, including the fact that the world best performances in running and cycling are equivalent to a VO_2 max of 89 ml O_2/kg/min and FTP of 6.4 Watts/kg.

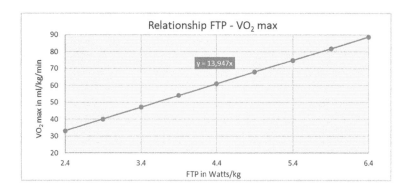

Others calibrate their power meters (also) with metabolic data of the VO_2 of test runners. The resulting power meter data match well with our universal theory.

Why are the results different?

At first sight we were quite puzzled by the different results. After discussions, we identified that theoretically there are 2 possible explanations for the differences:

1. *The Gross Metabolic Efficiency (GME)*

    Reference is made to fundamental research (e.g. Foss et al.[3]) indicating that muscle efficiencies may differ significantly, depending on the type of contractions (isometric, shorten, stretch, stretch-shorten). As a result the GME in running might be higher than 25%. However, we have gathered some literature data[4] on the GME of different sports that seems to confirm that 25% is the upper limit in running and cycling. Lower numbers are found in sports with larger turbulent losses, such as rowing, skiing, ice-skating and swimming. So, while we cannot rule out the possibility that the GME is higher in running than in cycling, this does not seem very likely.

2. *The elastic energy recovery in (muscles and) tendons)*

    The elastic energy recovery of the Achilles tendon and the lower leg muscles has been broadly discussed and acknowledged in literature. The

[3] M. L. Foss, S.J. Keteyian, Fox's physiological basis for exercise and sport, McGraw-Hill, 1998, ISBN 0-697-25904-8
[4] The Secret of Running, Hans van Dijk and Ron van Megen, available in several languages, in print and ebook, English print ISBN 978-1-78255-109-6

GME of various sports	
Walking	20-25%
Running	20-25%
Cycling	20-25%
Stepping	23%
Arm ergometry	16%
Arm and leg ergometry	18%
Rowing	10-20%
Skiing	10-15%
Slide-boarding	10-15%
Ice-skating	10-15%
Swimming	3-7%

Achilles tendon has a high capacity to store energy and this energy can be returned upon landing through elastic recoil. This recycling of energy would mean that in running the gross power could indeed be higher than in cycling as the recycled energy could be added to the net power of the human engine. This might be a good explanation why the force plates lead to higher power numbers than the metabolic data. Literature estimates that a return of the elastic energy of the Achilles tendon (and other tendons) may increase the positive mechanical work by some 25-30% (at no metabolic cost). So, all in all, this seems the most logical explanation for the differences.

For practical purposes this means that we can interpret the difference in numbers as the Net Running Power and the Gross Running Power, the difference being the Elastic Energy Recoil due to the Achilles tendon (and other tendons). Polar (and Garmin) choose to incorporate this elastic energy recoil in their power numbers.

Stryd power instead native Garmin or Polar running power?

Stryd offer IQ apps for Garmin. These IQ apps integrate great with Garmin's running watches and allow you to take full advantage of the features that Stryd offers. At Polar, you can also choose whether to use Polar Running Power or Stryd Power. For use during a race or workout you can put Stryd Power on a screen of your Polar.

To take advantage of the features of Stryd, it is necessary to additionally sync Stryd with your phone after the run. This pulls necessary information off the Stryd foot pod. For instance this is necessary in order to provide an accurate race prediction by Stryd.

Conclusions and outlook

We are very positive about the rapid developments in the field of running power. Competition brings better quality and lower cost, whereas new developments may lead the way to further improvements of the running power concept.

We hope that this chapter will shed some light on the (confusing) differences between the running power numbers and will help in channeling the discussions on the interpretation of the data.

Readers will understand that we prefer the physical and physiological approach of our Running Model as it offers the pre-eminent opportunity to evaluate and predict performances mathematically.

Good luck with your training and we wish you many personal bests to come!

Afterword

We've worked on the book The Power to Run: smart technology optimizes your performance with great pleasure and dedication.

Of course, new experiences will raise new questions and insights. We'll do everything we can to monitor these developments and continue to test and write about new developments. Stryd and other suppliers of running power meters will undoubtedly release updates that are worth investigating. And when a new power meter comes on the market, Hans and Ron will be among the first to test and compare it.

This afterword is not a word of thanks or a conclusion. It's the continuation of a great adventure that will last for years to come. An adventure where running through the woods with mud on your calves and your head in the wind meets scientific analysis and smart technology to analyze your workouts.

And if, after reading this book, you want to know more about power and the secrets of running, you can continue by reading the other books by Hans and Ron. The book The Secret of Running is available in print and as eBook, for sale in several languages.

We look forward to great events, fast times, and a lot of satisfaction.

Hans van Dijk
Ron van Megen
Koen de Jong

Hans van Dijk (1954) is emeritus professor and (together with Ron van Megen) author of The Secret of Running. He has been running since 1980 and has impressive PBs: for example, 31:55 on the 10K and 2:34:15 for the marathon. Hans is a walking encyclopedia and loves complicated formulas. Yet he can simplify complex concepts so that all can easily understand.

Ron van Megen (1957) studied Civil Engineering at the Technical University of Delft, just like Hans. Ron runs a bit slower than Hans with 39:30 on the 10K and 3:24:54 for the marathon but when it comes to organizing, forming partnerships and forging new plans, Ron is in the lead.

Koen de Jong (1979) is co-owner of the popular websites for runners sportrusten.nl and prorun. nl. He has written several books about running and respiration. His work has been translated into more than 10 languages and his marathon PB is in between that of Hans and Ron.

CPSIA information can be obtained
at www.ICGtesting.com
Printed in the USA
LVHW070003110422
715853LV00005B/35